How to Build a Writing Empire in 30 Days or Less

(The Work from Home Series: Book 2)

By

SAM KERNS

RainMaker
Press

Books by Sam Kerns

How to Work from Home and Make Money: 10 Proven Home-Based Businesses You can Start Today (Work from Home Series: Book 1)

How to Build a Writing Empire in 30 Days or Less (Work from Home Series: Book 2)

How to Start a Home-Based Food Business: Turn Your Foodie Dreams into Serious Income (Work from Home Series: Book 3) Coming Fall 2016

Thank you for buying

How to Build a Writing Empire in 30 Days or Less
(The Work from Home Series: Book 2)

Sign up at my website RainMakerPress.com for special offers, promotions, and information about new releases in this series.

Table of Contents

CHAPTER 1:

Why Being a Good Writer Just Isn't Enough Any More

The Big Lie

Let me guess—you're a talented writer who is willing to do whatever it takes to make a full-time living by writing. You've read countless articles and books on the subject, followed the suggestions in them, but you just can't seem to make the income leap. Or you may be a new writer who is convinced that you're missing something because your own experience just isn't matching up to what others say is possible. Or perhaps you've been moonlighting as a freelance writer for years, and you're convinced that it's simply not possible to quit your "real" job and do what you love full-time.

Let me tell you a secret. You've been lied to. Yes, you heard me correctly. **Lied. To.**

Our culture teaches us that if we work hard enough and have at least some talent, we can become a success and accomplish our dreams. I'm not necessarily disagreeing with that. In fact, I wholeheartedly believe in the American Dream. But what I am saying is that the freelance writing business isn't like most other career choices, and the uniqueness of the profession requires you to think a little outside of the box if you want to make a real living from it.

Take me as an example. I've considered myself a writer my entire life. When I was 10 years old, I knew that writing was the career—the only career—that I wanted. I took the first step when I reached my early twenties—after suffering miserably in an office environment for a few years—and sent queries to magazines and book publishers. (This was before it was possible to act as your own Indie publisher.) I was lucky because unlike many of my peers, I didn't seem to have any trouble landing assignments, and I was even given a book contract with a publisher in my second year.

But there was a problem. Despite my early success, I was nowhere near making what I needed to in order to earn a full-time living. I began to wonder what was wrong. I was working 50 to 60 hours a week, and even if I'd been able to secure more writing assignments, I wouldn't have had time to complete them. So instead of pursuing my writing dreams, I began to open other businesses, and while I achieved success with them, I couldn't let go of my desire to work as a writer. There had to be a way, the entrepreneur side of me said, but for the life of me, I couldn't figure it out.

Something certainly wasn't adding up.

The One Percent

Determined that it must be something I was doing wrong, I set out to find the solution. I read every book I could find about how to make a living as a freelance writer, but was dismayed to learn that I was already doing everything the books recommended. The "experts" on the subject suggested that I if I would only follow their time-proven plan, I'd be able to quit my day job in time and pursue my dream.

But that simply wasn't true. I was working hard and following all the expert advice, and I still wasn't earning an income large enough to support myself.

And then I came across a startling statistic that changed the course of my writing career and eventually led to this book. Are you sitting down?

Only about 10 percent of writers earn enough from working full-time to support themselves. *Ten percent.*

And the figures haven't improved over time. According to the Author's Guild, about half of the full-time writers they surveyed earn less than $12,000 a year in income, which falls below the federal poverty level. Not exactly what you had in mind when thinking about pursuing a writing career, is it?

And it's not much better in the U.K. According to a study commissioned by the Author's Licensing and Collecting Society, only 11.5 percent of freelancers who dedicate almost all of their time to writing earn enough money to support themselves.

Are you kidding me? What happened to doing our best and becoming a success? How about the fact that most writers end up working ridiculous hours just to keep up with the demand? What about that *American Dream?*

After I recovered from the shock, I became determined to uncover the secret of the ten percent. What made them so special? Were they that much above the cut in their skills? Did they have inside connections, or were they just plain lucky?

Here's what I found. A percentage of that ten percent are bestselling novelists, nonfiction writers who are experts in their field, or advertising and marketing copywriters who spent years building their reputation as the go-to person in sales copy.

The smallest portion of the ten percent are those writers who have managed to get in with the highest paying markets (sometimes thousands of dollars per article) and receive a steady flow of assignments from them. This generally takes years to accomplish.

But hey, what about the rest of the writers? Those who mostly work in the midrange markets and the internet? (In other words, the other 90 percent). Shouldn't they be able to make a decent living doing what they love, too?

That's when I discovered that it's all in the math.

It Just Doesn't Add Up

I decided to calculate how many hours I would have to write each month in order to earn a living that would afford me and my family a comfortable living. So I set a target income and worked backwards from there. My bottom line base figure was $100,000 per year. Yours might be different, and I encourage you to give this part of the process some serious thought.

First, add up your monthly obligations such as mortgage or rent, utilities, car payments, food, and the rest your living expenses. Don't forget to account for property taxes, insurance, college educations, and income taxes.

Next, you should add in the amount of money you want for savings, entertainment, and the amount of disposable income you'd be content with. Remember, we're not just talking about "making it." I want you to write down a figure that will comfortably sustain you and your family while putting money away for your retirement. As artists, we have to get a new mindset. The old thinking says that if you're lucky enough to do something you love, you will probably suffer financially. That's yesterday's thought process. I'm telling you, it is possible to do what you love AND make a good living.

Like I said, my target goal was $100,000, but yours should be individualized for your lifestyle. Now, take that number and divide it by 12, 52, and 260 (the average number of workdays in a year) to give you a rough idea of what you need to earn monthly, weekly, and daily. My $100,000 figure looks something like this:

Yearly Goal = $100,000
Monthly Goal = $8,333
Weekly Goal = $1,923
Daily Goal = $385

Next, I figured the average price customers pay per article. Now, this can be tricky because the rates are so diverse, depending on the level of experience of the writer and the type of article being assigned. For the purposes of this exercise, let's concentrate on internet content articles, as that's what most people will start out with in this business.

Typically, new writers start out at about $25 per article for internet content, and once they build a good portfolio, they can demand much higher rates. So, for this book, I'm going to assume that many of you are just starting out and use that rate. Please feel free to substitute your higher rate if you've already surpassed this level.

So, using the target goal of $100,000 and a $25 per article payout, here's what it looks like:

In order to earn $100,000 per year, you would have to produce 4,000 articles a year. That means you would have to write 333 article a month, or 83 a week. And if broken down into the 260 workdays in a year, that means in order to earn the target income, it would be necessary to write just over 15 articles a day.

Are you still with me? I know, it's discouraging and at this point, you might feel like it's not even possible. But good news is coming. Stay with me, okay?

Now that you understand how many articles it will take to get to your desired income, let's talk about how many hours you'll have to spend to write them.

Again, this will differ depending on your experience. A seasoned writer can complete an internet content article in a little under an hour, but a newbie may take two hours. Let's average that for our purposes, and use an hour and a half. Here's the amount of hours you would need to spend to meet the $100,000 per year goal.

- You would need to work 6,000 hours a year in order to write 4,000 articles a year.
- You would need to work 499.5 hours a month in order to write 333 articles a month.

- You would need to work 124.5 hours a week in order to write 83 articles a week.
- You would need to work 22.5 hours a day in order to write 15 articles a day.

Hang on, it's going to get worse before it gets better. (But remember, I have a solution.)

The Other Part of Writing

Let me break this to you gently: when working as a freelance writer, writing is only a portion of the tasks you'll need to complete every day in order to run a profitable business. And your other responsibilities? You guessed it. They're time consuming. Let's take a look at the other things you'll have to do in order to maintain your business.

Marketing

You will receive no assignments unless you sell yourself. We will go deeply into the how's and whys of marketing your writing Empire, but for now you should know that you will need to spend approximately two hours a day querying editors, bidding on jobs, looking for new clients, and managing your portfolio. So, you can automatically add two hours per day to all of the above figures.

Accounts Payable and Client Communications

Two other areas you will spend a great amount of time on are client communications and ensuring that you're paid for the jobs you've completed. Your clients will want to communicate with you before you begin work on an assignment in order to make sure you understand the scope of the project. Many of them will also want you to check in during the project so you can ask any questions you may have or update them on the status of the project. And once the project is completed, the client will either approve the work or ask you for modifications. Some clients are fine communicating via email, while others expect you to be available on Skype or even the phone.

Effective communication with clients is critical in order to establish long lasting business relationships. In other words, it will not only help you gain new clients, but it will also help you retain your hard earned accounts.

And once you've completed a project, you'll need to invoice the client, and then stay on top of that invoice until it's paid. All clients are different in how they want you to invoice them. Many use PayPal, while others prefer to put a check in the mail. Some will ask you to create a professional invoice, while others will simply ask you to email them an invoice. If the buyer hired you via your website, they will have paid your fee before you started the project. And if you work with clients on bid sites, each site has its own invoicing requirements that you'll need to learn.

So, how much time does all this take? Again, it depends on how many ongoing jobs you have and how many clients you work with, but it's safe to say that you should plan on about an hour and a half per day on these tasks.

Wait a minute. If we add three and a half hours to your workday for marketing, invoicing, and client communications, that means you'd have to work 26 hours a day to earn the target goal of $100,000 per year. That may be a problem, because the last time I checked, there were only 24 hours in a day.

That's not something all those other how-to writing books spend a lot of time on, is it? But now that I've uncovered the problem, we can talk about the solution. And there *is* a solution.

Thinking like a Twenty-First Century Writer

At this point, you must realize that there are simply not enough hours in the day to do all it takes to earn a real living as a full-time freelance writer. Time is the enemy. It's the number one reason so many writers spend years struggling on an "artist's" income (Sorry, but there's nothing romantic about that when you're trying to support a family), or end up taking a "day job" in order to help ends meet. If you're already a freelancer, how many times have you wished you could clone yourself several times over to be able to produce more content so you could earn a decent living?

Exactly.

What if I told you that you could double, triple, or even quadruple your time, allowing you to not only increase your income, but also spend more time pursuing the types of writing projects *you* want to?

What I'm talking about is building a writing Empire—an organization of writers that all work for you under your direction. I'm talking about taking your passion, your skill, and making big business out of it. I'm talking about transforming the way you get business and the way you produce it.

I'm taking about finally bringing the freelance writing industry into the twenty-first century.

SAM KERNS

This is not just an idea—it's something I've done myself for years, and it transformed my professional life in a matter of months.

It can transform your world, too.

Read on and let me show you a step-by-step plan you can use to build your own writing Empire.

After all, why should the big boys have all the fun?

CHAPTER 2:

You are the Ruler. What Kind of Empire do You Want to Build?

So, what do you think? Are you ready to take the steps needed to accelerate your career? Are you ready to jump in and make a real go at your dreams? I assume that if you've begun this chapter, the answer is yes. Great—I hope to see you succeed. But before you dive in, there are some things you need to consider.

You see, not every Empire is the same, and you now have the unique privilege of designing yours from scratch. From the bottom up. A custom made blueprint of your dreams. **Your** very own Empire.

Let's get to it, shall we?

Build the Foundation of Your Empire

Some of you may be striving to make the Fortune 500 list, while others may desire to earn enough money to support their family while doing what they love. Even others might intend to build a family business they can leave to their children when they pass on or retire. Whatever is driving you, I assume that most of you are trying to get to a place where you have the means and the time to carve out a life where you can pursue the things that matter the most to you. And it's important that you identify those things while you're in the planning stages of your business.

If you don't build your Empire intentionally, you'll soon find that your business is managing you instead of the other way around. And that's just no fun for anyone.

The business structure I'm going to lay out for you in this book is a rapidly expanding model, so please don't skips any of the steps, including this one.

Now, put your dream cap on—it's time to start building your Empire.

What are Your Priorities?

Webster defines a priority as something that is more important than other things and needs to be dealt with first. In other words, the priorities you set must come first in your life. The difficulty lies in the fact that not everyone's priorities are the same. Some people's may look like this:

Faith
Family
Career
Personal time

While other's may look more like this:

Career
Bank account
Personal time
Material possessions

How you set your priorities will not only determine how much time you put into your business, but also how it's structured. For example, will it always come first, or will you design it around your family's needs? Your priorities will also dictate how quickly you plan to grow. In other words, if it's number four on your priority list, you should build your Empire slowly and methodically, but if it's number one, you should plan to bolt right out of the gate.

This may seem obvious to you, but you would be amazed at the number of people who fail to identify their priorities in the planning stages of their business, and then get stuck with a business that doesn't fit their desired lifestyle. Don't let that happen to you.

Instead, quickly jot down the top five priorities in your life, and then think about them for a while. Put them in order of what matters most to you so you'll have an idea of how to build the foundation of your new business.

Set Your Goals

What's your number one reason for wanting to start a business? That's your goal. Is it money? If so, then every decision you make when planning your business should be made with the goal of making money.

Or is it to get to a point where you have the time and financial stability to finally get serious about that novel? Then that should drive your plans. Is your goal to make a real living while staying home with your children? Then let that be the motivation behind all of your planning decisions. Remember, no two businesses are the same, and the key to the successful ones is that the owner planned for it.

Don't forget that you're planning an Empire that YOU will rule. This is the stage where you can determine the exact type of Empire you'll have. Take a moment and solidify your number one goal in your mind, and then write it down at the bottom of the list you made in the last section.

Blend Your Priorities and Goals

Here's where it gets a little tricky. Life is weird and sometimes our priorities and goals don't match up. For instance, let's say that you're a single mom whose priority is your kids, but your goal is to make a lot of money. Can it be done? Sure, with some serious planning and compromise.

Or maybe you're a business executive whose priority is to make sure your family stays in the comfortable lifestyle your corporate job allows, but your goal is to have more time for yourself. Can it be done? Yep. But it's going to take a lot of thought, planning and compromise.

So, how do you blend seemingly incompatible priorities and goals?

Let's start by looking at the example of the single mom. Since her kids are her priority, it's probably safe to assume that she'll want to spend a good portion of her time with them. But we all know that if you want to make the big bucks, you'd better be willing to put in the hours, right?

Not always.

With some specific income goal planning, this single mom could completely control her work hours and income, while doggedly working toward her big picture. Her plans may be on a two year, four year, or even a five year projection depending on the age of her children, but what will ensure her success is the process of mapping out her plan and then sticking to it.

Stop for a moment and think about your priorities and goals. Are they compatible? If so, you're one of the lucky ones. But if you're like most people, they're not. In that case, I want you to pick up a pen (or a keyboard) and begin to make some notes about what compromises might bring them closer together, and how long range planning might make them work together. Be sure to include any time delays or income adjustments that you know are in your future. Once you've brainstormed, we'll move on to the next section.

And don't worry if you get stuck at this part of the planning stage. Later in the book, we'll talk about specific timelines for this business, and how they'll play into your goals.

How Many Writers Should You Hire?

In chapter one, you determined the amount of money you want to earn in your business. You also saw that it's highly unlikely—in fact impossible—for you to get there by yourself.

Let's do something about that.

For the following exercises, I'm going to continue

to use the figure of $100,000. In fact, I'll use it for the entire course of this book to make things easier, but feel free to substitute your own figure and compute along with me.

A good internet article writer can generally produce 6-10 articles a day. Let's average that and use 8 a day for this exercise, or about 176 per month using 22 workdays per month. Keep in mind that your writers won't usually start out producing that many articles unless you hire seasoned writers, but it shouldn't take new writers very long to get up to speed.

Okay, knowing that each of your writers can produce about 40 articles per week, let's talk about how many you need to hire to reach your goal. But first there's one important thing we haven't yet discussed, and it will definitely affect your bottom line: how much you'll need to pay the writers for their work.

How Much Do I Pay My Writers?

Writer's fees for internet content are all over the map. You'll find some writers who are willing to work for $5 an article and others who wouldn't dream of doing it for less than $50 per article—or even more. You goal is to find those writers who will accept a lesser price for articles in exchange for constant, ongoing work. Now, having said that, I believe it's important to pay your writers a living wage. I've seen some people try to hire writers while offering them a ridiculous amount of money. That only breeds discontent and sloppy work.

You probably won't pay all of your writers the same amount for articles. Some will turn in work that needs a good amount of editing, and you should pay them at the bottom end of your scale. Others will turn in perfect work, and you should do all you can to keep them happy, including paying them a rate that's at the top end of your scale.

As a general rule, you should plan to pay your writers about 40 percent of what you're paid on the project. And since you're going to look for clients who will pay you a minimum of $25 per article, that means you should set your pay rate at $10.00 or less per article. While it's true that the writer is spending about an hour or so for each article, you are the one who will be looking for the work, making sure the articles are ready for publication, communicating with the clients, and following through on the invoicing. You're also the one who will take the chance of not being paid. While it rarely happens, sometimes clients don't pay, but that doesn't mean you can withhold payment from the writer. It just means you would take a loss on the job. (Again, this is rare, and we'll go into ways to prevent it from happening in a later chapter.)

So, using a figure of $10 per article for your writer's rates, here are some numbers that show you how many writers you'll need to hire in order to reach $100,000 per year.

- If a writer produces 40 articles per week, your gross sales (at $25 an article) from the writer are $1,000 per week, $4,000 per month, or $48,000 per year.
- If you pay the writer $10 per article, you will owe them $400 per week, $1,600 per month, or $19,200 per year.

- Your net profit from that writer is $600 per week (at a profit of $15 per article), $2,400 per month, or $28,800 per year.
- If your goal is $100,000 per year, you would need to hire three and a half writers to meet it. ($100,000 divided by $28,800 = 3.5)

Now, obviously, every writer isn't going to work for the same rate per article, or be able to produce the same amount of articles per week, but this exercise should give you a general idea of many writers you will need to hire in order to make your yearly income goal.

Is That Much Work Available?

I know some of you are thinking there is no way there is that much work up for grabs. I'm here to tell that there is. There are currently about one billion websites online, and the one thing they all have in common is the need for content. We'll dig deeply into the best way to tap into all that available work later, but for now, rest assured that there is an overabundance of work to be had.

Let's Start Building

At the beginning of this book, I promised you that I would show you how to build your writing Empire in 30 days or less, right? That means the clock is ticking. Let's start off by talking about the basics so you'll have all the information you'll need in order to begin construction on your new Empire.

Empire Builders Arch Enemy #1: Vagueness in your goals.

Remember, a goal is your number one reason for building your writing Empire. It's what will motivate you, keep you going, and push you in times of confusion and uncertainty.

For that reason, your goal must be crystal clear in your mind. If it's not, stop right now and make it that way before you go on to the next chapter.

CHAPTER 3:

Under Construction. What You'll Need to Build Your Empire

Fortunately, building a writing Empire won't take a lot of specialized equipment and software, but there are some things you simply must have. Let's take a brief look at the necessities.

A Computer

The most important piece of equipment you'll need is a computer—and a good one. You'll use it to find and communicate with clients and writers, seek new jobs, send invoices, and more. I've found that Word documents are typically most compatible with client and writer needs, so I recommend getting a PC and not a Mac. (Although you could probably make either one work)

The Ability to Communicate

You'll need to be available to both clients and your writers, and everyone has a preferred method of communication. At the very least, you should have a phone with you at all hours of the day, and well as the ability to chat on Skype or other forms of instant messaging.

Plagiarism Software

Do not, I repeat, do not skip this item. We will discuss the issue of writer plagiarism in depth later, but for now, suffice it to say that skipping plagiarism checks on your incoming work could easily take down your Empire in a day. There is specialized software that can check a writer's work against all other online content, and if a writer cuts and pasts an existing article and then turns it in to you as their own work (yes, this does happen), the software will instantly catch it.

There are a few great plagiarism checkers online that you can use, and you should test each of them to find out which one you're most comfortable working with. For example, you can use Plagiarisma, a free checker, NoPlag, which is a paid option ranging from $4.99 to $29.99, depending on how many checks you do a month, or PlagTracker, which costs about $7.50 per month. (The site also has a free version, but you will be limited in how often you can use it. It's a great way to try the service, though.) Do your research and subscribe to the best program you can afford.

Invoicing and Payment Methods

In a future chapter, I'll teach you the mechanics of

invoicing your clients and getting paid, but you will need to establish your system before you bid on the first job. Because you will likely have clients from all over the world, you will need a system that allows instant invoicing half a world away, currency exchange, and a way to accept credit cards. In addition, you'll need a system that allows you to manage refunds and allows you to quickly and easily pay your writers. Finally, this system should help you keep track of all the transactions for your monthly reports and evaluations, which will also make income tax time easier.

I've found the best way to handle my billing and payment needs is with an online service. Now there are a few to choose from, but in my experience, PayPal is the easiest because not only does it provide me with everything I listed above, but it's also the service most of your clients and writers will likely already use.

PayPal offers a few different options for users. You can create a personal account and link your bank account and credit card to it and use them to pay your writers. When doing this, you should always check the box that indicates you are paying for goods or services so that the writer—not you—will be responsible for the processing fee.

On the other hand, when your clients pay you, you will be the one to pay the fee. It will be deducted from your balance, so be sure to figure that into your bids.

If you want the ability to accept credit cards (and you should), you'll need to move up to the business plan. With it, you'll be able to accept all the major credit cards, and that privilege will cost you an additional 2.9 percent, plus a .30 cent fee per transaction.

Not every client will want to pay you with PapPal, so it's important to be prepared with other options. (In fact, I prefer that clients don't pay me that way because of the fees. But I always offer it as an option.) Some clients will want to use automatic deposits, especially those clients you do repeat business with month after month. And many will prefer to pay you by check. Finally, you should also have a shopping cart set up on your website so clients can easily order work from you.

For the clients who want you to invoice them, you can either create invoices in Word or other software, you can make use of PayPal's invoicing system, or use another online invoicing system. Some of your options are Due.com, where you can send 3 invoices a month for free, Freshbooks, where you'll get a free 30-day trial, and then pay $19.95 per month, or Zoho, where it's free for under five clients, and $15 per month for more.

Keep in mind that your writers will need to invoice you for their work because they will be working as independent contractors and not employees. You can easily get in hot water with the IRS if you blur the lines between employees and independent contractors, so insist on receiving invoices from them before they're paid. We'll discuss this issue in depth later, but for now, remember that you should never pay one of your writers unless they've first invoiced you.

An Online Portfolio

Anyone you want to do business with is going to want to see samples of your work. And while many writers simply email potential clients a sample or two of their work, you'll want to go the extra step. After all, you're building an Empire, not just a regular writing business.

By creating a professional online portfolio of your work, you'll not only set yourself apart, but potential clients will be able to view various styles of your work, get a feel for the types of article you offer, and they can do this in one convenient place. In the next chapter, we'll discuss the concept of creating your business identity and branding, and your website and online portfolio should be an extension of that brand.

But for now, you should begin checking out a few freelance writer sites to get a feel of how they're put together. You can google "freelance writer's websites" to see a few great examples. Look them over, and then start dreaming about your own site.

And don't forget to dream big.

Here's a brief overview of how build your own website, which will contain your online portfolio.

The Basics of Building a Website

You don't have to spend a lot of money to create a professional looking site that buyers will appreciate. Here's how to make use of some free and inexpensive tools to create your own stunning portfolio.

Purchase and Register Your Domain Name

Now that you have a business name, it's time to put it on the internet map. You do this by registering a domain name (the address of your website) with a company and then paying a small fee for the exclusive rights to use it. Registering a domain name is an easy process.

There are a lot of new extensions for sale such as

.net, .biz and many others, but if you want the best success, you should stick with the tried and true .com extension. But some studies show that over 99 percent of the dictionary has been used in .com names, so finding an available name isn't going to be easy.

The best case scenario is to use your business name in your website address. For instance, I choose to use my publishing name, Rainmaker Press for my website. It's simple, easy and conveys what I want people to understand about what I'm selling. I got lucky that no one else registered this name before I did, but that's not always the case.

If your business name isn't available when you register your domain name, you should keep these factors in mind:

- **Keep it short.** Don't fall into the trap of using a long domain name just so you can include your business name. People won't remember it and it comes across as salesy and unprofessional.

- **Don't use hyphens.** Sometimes people add a hyphen to still be able to use their business name if it's already taken. For example, my name was already taken for samkerns.com. I could have used a hyphen and registered sam-kerns.com, but what would have happened is people would have ignored or forgot the hyphen and ended up at someone else's site.

- **Don't use keywords for SEO.** In times past, website owners could just keywords in their domain names and Google would point people to their site when they searched for the word. For instance, before Googles' recent algorithm changes, it would have been smart to call my website workfromhome.com. But because of the changes Google has made, they don't reward those kinds of domain names anymore.

- **Use a .com extension.** We discussed this in an earlier paragraph, but I don't want you to miss it, so I decided to also include it on this list. If your business name is taken as a .com domain, it can be tempting to register it with another extension, but don't. People trust .com extensions and automatically use them when searching for a site. Using another extension can result in missed business and a lack of trust for your website from the public.

Now that you know the basics of how to register a domain name, you'll need to know where to do it. My favorite domain registration company is GoDaddy. They offer a promotional offer of .99 cents for one year, and folks, it just doesn't get any cheaper than that. You can also find .99 cent registration fees at 1&1,

Choose a Web Hosting Company

Now that you have your domain name registered, you'll need to contract with a web hosting company to park it. You can hire a website designer for thousands of dollars to create your website, figure out how to build it yourself, or you can do it the easy way. And since we're talking about opening an online store with the least amount of effort, I want to talk about the easiest and most affordable way to do it.

The cheapest way to open an online store is to use an ecommerce platform that allows you build a website by clicking and dragging (no experience necessary), and the ability to collect payments online. There are many of these sites to choose from, and the prices vary. Here's a rundown of the most common ones.

- Wix. This host allows you to build a customized ecommerce site with a payment gateway and shopping cart for $16.58 per month.

- Weebly. If you don't need to collect payments on your site, (for instance if you sell books on Amazon, and can direct them there), you can set up a fully customized site for free. If you want to allow customers to purchase directly from you, it will cost $25 per month for an ecommerce package that includes a shopping cart. Shopping carts allow your customers to pay you with credit cards or via PayPal.

- Shopify. This is another easy-to-use site that offers a low rate. Prices start at $9 per month for one buy button (if you only have one product), and $29 per month for a full online store.

- BigCommerce. This host offers an all-inclusive website with all the tools you need starting at $29 per month.

- Squarespace. This host now offers ecommerce sites that have an integrated shopping cart and other important essentials. Plans start at $26 per month, and you won't have to sign a contract.

- WordPress via BlueHost. If you have a little more skill, you can set up a WordPress site using BlueHost. It will host your WordPress site for as little as $3.49 per month. Then you can use WooCommerce to install a free shopping cart.

When building your website, it's important to keep your future customers in mind. Make it easy for them by clearly defining what each page will do by titling it appropriately. For your online portfolio, you will probably only need a Portfolio page where you show off samples of your work, an About Us page, where you highlight your company's brand, a Contact Me page so customers can get in touch, and a blog, which you will use to draw new customers to your site by the use of keywords.

Collecting Payments

If you want to offer customers more options to pay you, you'll need to take an additional couple of steps. First, you'll need to set up an internet merchant account, which enables you to receive the funds once a customer has made a purchase. You can usually set up this type of account at your local bank, or by using a merchant account provider. These third party vendors transfer the funds to your bank. Here are two to choose from:

- Network Solutions. This provider has plans starting at just $9.95 per month.

- MerchantPlus. Starting costs for this provider are $30 per month.

Next, you'll need to use a payment gateway which is how your store is connected to your internet merchant account. Payment gateways transfer your customer's sensitive data into your merchant account in a secure way. If you use a bank for your merchant account, it may provide the gateway, but if not, you can investigate these alternatives:

- Authorize. You'll pay a $49 set up fee, $25 a month and a 2.9 percent plus .30 cent transaction fee for each sale.

- eWay. There is no sign up or monthly fee with this gateway provider, and you'll only pay 2.9 percent plus a .30 cent transaction fee for each sale.

Make Sure Your Site is Secure

Most consumers won't buy from a site that doesn't offer encryption of their credit cards and other payment information. In order to run a successful online store, you'll need a Secure Socket Layer (SSL) certificate to convince your shoppers that their information is safe.

You have options when it comes to securing your site, and those options vary in price. For starters, you may already have a third party SSL certificate from your ecommerce platform if you use sites like Weebly and Wix. Your site won't have the certificate, but the third party sites where the transactions are done, such as PayPal, have them so your customers are protected. However, if you use Shopify to build your site, an SSL certificate is included in the price.

If you build the site yourself using WordPress and BlueHost, you can purchase an SSL certificate from Symantec for about $400 per year, SSLMate for $15.95 per year, or sign up for a free certificate that has to be renewed every 90 days from Let's Encrypt. The last option is a little more work, but hey, the goal here is low cost, right?

Believe it or not, but that's all the equipment and specialized software you'll need to build your Empire. Stop and think about that for a minute. We're talking about a business that you can build and earn a livable wage on, and if you already own a decent computer, you're startup costs are zilch. Zero. Nada. Yes, you'll have some monthly or one off fees for things like plagiarism software and credit card processing fees, but that's just a part of doing business. Your startup costs on the other hand are nothing.

Okay, take a deep breath and let's move on. In the next chapter, we'll talk about creating the identity of your Empire.

Empire Builders Arch Enemy #2: Not Having Your Back-End Systems Set up Before Launching

I know you're in a hurry to get your business off the ground, but it would be a huge mistakes to launch your business without already having the tools and systems that we talked about in place. Don't be tempted to hurry past this important aspect of building your foundation. Instead, get your back end systems set up so your projects, client communications and everything else will run smoothly and flawlessly.

CHAPTER 4:

Establish Your Empire's Identity

I want you to do a quick exercise: take a look at these three names and think about what comes to mind:

- American Express Platinum Card
- Kraft Macaroni and Cheese
- Travelocity

Finished? Let me guess, when you thought about the American Express Platinum Card, you instantly felt a sense of wealth and an extravagant lifestyle, and you might have even conjured up an image of a yacht or two. Am I close? But why? After all, when you get right down to it, isn't a credit card just a credit card? Why don't you think of yachts when you think about a Capitol One card or regular green American Express card? One reason: branding.

What about Kraft macaroni and cheese? If you're like most people, you thought of kids and family. But do you get the same images when you think of Velveeta macaroni and cheese? No? That's because even though the products are similar, their branding concepts aren't. Kraft = kids and family. Velveeta = a hearty meal.

Finally, when you thought about Travelocity, an image of a gnome probably popped into your mind and it gave you a sense of playfulness. Yep, that's exactly how the company planned it because it's the image or brand their marketing experts decided they wanted to portray.

Do you see the significance of creating a brand for your own Empire? Or do you just want to be another writing company among the others in the sea of internet sites? I didn't think so.

Let's figure out how you can apply this important marketing technique to help you brand and build your Empire.

Why Branding is Key in the Planning Stages

Establishing the brand—or identity—of your business intentionally in the planning stages of your Empire will allow you to present a solid, united front to the world. Remember, as the ruler of your Empire, you get to define how the world at large perceives your business and its services. Do you want them to think of you as a fun, quirky business that is up to any challenge, or a serious business that rejects more assignments than it receives? Do you want clients to think you have a huge waiting list, or is your preferred image that of a no nonsense general writing business that is quick to take an assignment and get it completed? None of these images or brands is better than the other, but all will attract a different type of client, so it's important to really think about how you want your business to be perceived. Let me give you a few reasons why this matters so much.

Let's imagine that you've branded yourself as a writing business that has a talent for making almost any article fun. You've emphasized this type of corporate personality in your web portfolio, and everything else you use to market your business.

But in your assignment searches, you find that you're consistently denied the higher paying professional or scientific types of articles and projects. Why? Because you're branded yourself out of the market. A high-end businessman looking for a serious ghost blogger for his personal blog probably wouldn't hire someone who markets their writing as fun. It would be akin to serving Kraft macaroni and cheese at a Fortune 500 corporate event.

Are you getting the picture? Let's try another one.

Imagine that you've created the brand of an elite writing business that anyone would be lucky to be able to hire. You charge exorbitant rates because…well, you're worth it. You are, in essence, the Platinum Card of writing companies.

But one month business is down, so you bid on a job that isn't exactly high caliber and the pay rate is nowhere near your norm. Would it be a surprise to you if you didn't get the job? In circumstances like these, the potential client might think you were either overqualified or a fake.

Perhaps you've noticed that I keep stressing intentional branding. Let me show you an example of what can happen when a writer allows themselves to be unintentionally branded.

Imagine a new writing company just starting out that accepts any and all assignments. Now, there's nothing wrong with that. In fact, most of you will do just that in the building stages of your Empire. But this person shows no discretion in what or how he displays his work in his online portfolio or other marketing efforts. Once this budding entrepreneur has built a foundation, he begins to think about which direction he wants to take his business in. Perhaps he's found that his specialty is medical writing and he wants to establish his business as the go-to place for that type of writing. Is it too late for him? After all, he would have to unbrand himself as a Jack-of-all-trades writer and re-brand himself as a medical writer. Is it impossible? Maybe so, maybe not.

But wouldn't it have been easier if he had intentionally branded himself all along by controlling what went in his portfolio and marketing materials?

Okay, now that you understand the seriousness of intentionally branding your Empire, let's take a look at some things you'll need to consider.

Will You Present Yourself as an Individual or a Company?

Potential clients will either think of you as a company of writers, or as an individual, and as far as branding yourself, this is one of the most important decisions you'll make. Why? It will determine how the world (your clients) relate to your business. Will they see you as a personality or as an entity—a business that merely serves a function.

Once again, let's look to established businesses to make the point. Consider these two big names in the DIY industry: Martha Stewart and Hobby Lobby. I bet if you're a fan of Martha Stewart, you almost feel as if you know her. You think she's brilliant and warm and you wouldn't hesitate to invite her over for a cup of tea so you could compare fabric swatches and talk about colors. On the other hand, Hobby Lobby offers much of the same products that Martha does, but you likely view that business as a source—a great supplier of the things you need. Do you see the difference?

You will have to decide which type of relationship you want to develop with your clients: a pull up a chair and chat type, or a polite but keep it at arm's length distance kind. Neither one is better than the other, but the one you choose will be the basis for the remainder of your branding decisions.

It will also determine which type of clients you attract to your business. Do you plan to specialize in family or gardening topics? Then you might consider branding yourself as a warm and fuzzy individual. Or will you aggressively pursue the business market as your main source of income? It wouldn't be wise, in that case, to feature a photo of you and your kids at Disneyland on your portfolio page. Instead, you'd do better to present a corporate image.

If you've decided to brand yourself as an individual, you have another decision to make.

Decide on a Gender

Now that's a strange title for this section, isn't it? But if you're going to build your Empire's brand with purpose, you need to consider everything.

If you're a woman, have you ever felt at a disadvantage because you think it's a man's world? Now's your time to get even. Or maybe you're a man who has been trying to break into writing for a topic typically dominated by women. Don't despair. It is possible to brand yourself as either a female or male in order to get the market share you want.

Think about it—there are products which, quite frankly, could be used by either males or females, but they've been branded one way or another. Take soap, for example. Last time I checked, both men and women use soap, and there are essentially the same ingredients in most bars. But the marketers of Dove, a mild, fragrant white bar of soap, have clearly chosen women as their target audience. Just look at their branding. The soft colors they use and the fact that they call their soap bars beauty bars appeal to women. But isn't the soap good for men, too? I'm sure it would clean their skin just as well, but when is the last time you saw the neighborhood bachelor loading up on Dove beauty bars?

Well, what of it? Is it an accident? Nope. It's the direct effect of intentional branding.

Let's imagine that you've decided to brand yourself as an individual, but you're concerned that you'll have an uphill climb because you're a woman who wants to specialize in sports medicine articles. You'd be right to worry because you would probably have to spend a lot of time proving yourself in a field typically dominated by men. In that case, you may consider branding yourself as a male. What? I can hear some of you asking if that's dishonest. Of course not. Is the Philsbury doughboy real?

I know a woman who wrote under a man's name for years, and she says it's the most fun she's ever had. Remember, your goal in branding your Empire is to create the image that will attract the types of clients you want.

However you design your site and portfolio, a potential client will likely have a general idea of whether you're a male or female. Hey, we live in a male/female world, and that makes it difficult to not view things from that perspective. Be aware of it, and then be intentional in your design.

That's fine, you might say, but I've decided to brand my Empire as a company and not an individual. You have some decisions to make as well. What colors will you use? Photos? Will you present yourself as a formal business or a company with a more informal attitude? What fonts will you use to portray your intended image?

Should You Use a Pen Name or Not?

This dilemma may already be solved for those of you who have decided to write under a different gender or brand yourself as a company, but there are bound to be some of you thinking about bylines.

Many people write under a different name for their internet work for one reason: they want to keep their internet content work separate from their other writing. So here's my advice: if you aspire to be a novelist or any other type of "serious" writer, you should probably use a pen name for internet content. The only exception would be serious articles that would contribute to your desired outcome. For example, if your ultimate goal is to write books about dogs, think about using your real name for any articles about that subject.

Your Prices Contribute to Your Brand

Do you want to know a secret? Come closer and I'll whisper it in your ear because I really don't want too many people to know about it. Are you listening?

You can set your own prices. Your own prices. And no, I'm not kidding you.

Remember how you decided whether your image would be corporate or individual? Male or female? Quirky or serious? Now it's time for another decision. Do you want to charge on the low, mid-range, or higher end of the pricing scale for your content?

Now, before you automatically say the high end, you should know that there some other factors that you have to consider before making a decision—some of which you probably haven't thought of. Here they are in a nutshell.

Charging on the High End

If you're going to charge on the high end, you'd better be able to back it up. In other words, you have to know your limitations. Think about it, why would some markets or specialty clients pay more? It's simple. They expect a higher grade of writing. Be honest about your abilities (and those of your writers), because nothing can take down an Empire faster than work not up to the expectations of clients. There are rating systems, reviews, and online forums where buyers can go to talk about their experiences with your company, and if too many of them leave negative feedback you may as well pull up the draw bridge and buckle down because it will be a long time before your next assignment.

On the other hand, if you have the experience and know how, by all means, charge as much as you can get away with. It will obviously result in more income for less work, which should be the goal of any Empire builder.

Charging on the Low End

Some people approach this from the opposite end of the spectrum. They low bid every job and produce thousands of low paying internet content articles every month—and they're paid as little as $5 per article. I know I promised that I wouldn't torture you with any more math, but please allow me one small digression to make an important point.

If you hire overseas writers (much more about this later) and pay them $2.50 per article, while charging your clients $5 per article, your numbers could look something like this:

- Twelve and a half writers turning in 40 articles per week equals 2,000 articles per month.
- 2,000 articles per month at $5 per article equals $10,000 in gross income for you.
- If you pay the writers $2.50 per article, that leaves you with $5,000 per month, or $60,000 per year in income.

Is there enough internet content jobs to supply you with this amount of work? Yes, and I know that because I've done it. Taking this route will result in more work for you because you will have to heavily edit the articles (we'll talk about a solution for that later), but it is more than possible.

So, the next time you see those $5 article job postings, don't laugh so hard. These types of clients aren't looking for first rate writing, but instead their goal is content that will draw visitors to their site by the use of keywords.

What's more, it typically only takes an experienced internet content writer about 20 minutes to produce one. That's because they're not serious pieces, but formulas designed to draw people to a website. Yes, Google has changed its algorithms to discourage keyword stuffing and poorly written articles, but there are still plenty of people who want this type of content.

If you don't mind a hectic pace and don't have an issue with "writer's pride," this may be your ticket.

Charging Mid-Range Prices

Mid-range fees are what most of you will decide to charge. By starting out in the mid-range area, you'll easily be able to adjust your prices up or down as the market demands. Unless your branding image requires a specific range like the one we just talked about, it's probably best that you start out here.

Market Research

Now that you've made some pretty hefty decisions about the shaping of your Empire's identity, you ought to be feeling pretty good about yourself. But before you finalize your decision, there's one more thing I want you to do. Take another look at those writer's websites I had you look up earlier and scope out your competition. Are there any that have branded themselves too similarly to what you had in mind? If so, you'd better make a few adjustments. Is there an obvious lack of high-end or low-end writers? No one branding themselves as the financial writer like you had in mind? Or are there already ten of them?

Now, take your market research a little further and engage with the competition. Ask for price quotes and maybe hire a couple of them to see what kind of quality they produce. Be sure to keep careful notes about what you liked and didn't like from each of your future competitors.

After you've thoroughly checked out the competition, you may need to adjust your plan accordingly, depending on what you find. Remember, you want your Empire to stand out as unique even if you intend to brand yourself as a mid-range, general writer.

Your Brand: Get a Visual

Now it's time to take everything and consolidate it into an easy to use visual that will help you visualize your brand. I call it brand charting, and it's the last step in the process. Here are some examples of what it looks like.

The first example represents a brand for the low end market. Its purpose is to make buyers feel like they'll get good content fast and inexpensively. It looks like this:

> **Name: Crank 'Em Out Writing Services**
> **Price range:** Low-end
> **Style:** Company branding that is young and hip
> **Colors:** Orange, blue and white to portray crisp and fast writing

And here's another one in the mid-range market that is designed to convey trustworthiness:

Sam Green Reliable Writing Services
Price range: Mid-range
Style: Individual branding that appeals to male and female clients because it's friendly and conveys trust.
Colors: Green and tan to portray nature, friendliness, and all-inclusiveness

Finally, here's an example of a high-end specialty writing company:

The Professional Medical Writing Group
Price range: high-end
Style: Company branding with a gender neutral professional image. The name clearly identifies this company as one that specializes in medical writing.
Colors: Blue and gold to highlight its upper end prices and professionalism.

Now it's time to use all the hard work you've done in this chapter and fill in your own visual branding chart so you can get a visual of your new company and see it as your potential clients will. Use the spaces below to create your own branding chart.

Name:
Price range:
Style:
Colors:

Keep Your Branding Consistent

What would you think if you walked into a McDonalds and the color scheme was hunter green and purple? What is you saw a pale pink Starbucks? A Hallmark commercial that wasn't warm and fuzzy? Here's an even better one. What if you looking to hire a writer, and after looking at dozens of sites, finally found one that you connected with. Not only was their writing and prices just right for your project, but their web portfolio, as well as all the other interactions you'd had with them, gave you confidence. It was the colors they used and their overall branding that made you feel like they were just the right company for your Special Project.

And then, just as you were about to hire them to do the work, you received an email from them. You open it, expecting to see the calming blue and green serene motif you'd seen every other time you communicated with them, but instead of the soothing brand you'd grown to expect, you see this:

> Wow!! Have We Got a Deal for You!!!!!!
> It's been a loooooong time since we've offered a discount, but we're just so dog-gone sure you could use one, we decided to make an exception.

The email was a blinding black, white and red with extra large letters that made you feel as if it was shouting at you. Might you think twice about awarding them the project? After all, who needs a schizophrenic writer?

Perhaps the one thing that's more important to the foundation of your Empire than branding is *consistency* in your branding. In every communication or contact you make with the outside world, you must present your brand's image.

Promise me you won't ever get lazy and try to cut corners, or say "I'll depart from my brand just this once," when it comes to your company's image. Not ever. Okay?

Empire Builders Arch Enemy #3: A Failure to Differentiate Yourself with Your Brand.

If there is one thing you should have learned from this chapter, it's that you need to stand out from the crowd when it comes to having a successful writing Empire. And luckily, you are the one who gets to decide how you will present your company to the world. What will make you memorable in the eyes of your clients? Hone in on that, and never allow yourself to be thought of as just another writing business. Instead, use your unique branding to stand out in a world of sameness.

CHAPTER 5:

Putting up Road Signs and Getting the Word out About Your Empire

Now that you understand how important it is to brand your company and have hopefully have tinkered with an idea or two, we need to discuss the vital role that sales and marketing will play in the success of your Empire. But first, let's clear up a common area of confusion.

The Difference Between Branding and Marketing

Many people confuse branding and marketing and think of them as the same thing. But they're not. Here are their official definitions.

- **To brand** a business is to mark it with a brand.

- **Branding** is the marketing of products by connecting them with a popular brand name.

- **Marketing** is the total of activities involved in the moving of goods from the producer to the consumer, including but not limited to selling and advertising.

As you can see, even though branding and marketing are inexplicitly linked together, they are separate acts. If I may be so bold as to paraphrase Webster, to brand a company is to attach a unique mark or impression on it. To market that business is to use that unique mark or impression in your advertising in order to make the consumer want to purchase your product.

See the difference? Now you can see why it's necessary to determine your brand *before* you begin to market your business. Okay, now that you understand this critical point, let's talk about getting the word out about your Empire. We'll start with one of the most misunderstood options out there. If you can nail this one, you'll go a long way in building a strong foundation for your Empire.

Bid Sites

The World Wide Web is a huge place, and your job is to make sure your presence is known on it. Most people in the market for a writer will go there to find one, and I'm going to show you how to make it easy for them to find you.

The first place to begin putting up road signs that point to your Empire is on the various job and bid sites. This is where the bulk of your business will come from. But if you think it's just a matter of placing bids on as many projects as you can find, you'd better think again. Bidding on jobs is an art, and once you master it, you will indeed have the keys to your Empire.

But before we begin talking about how to use these sites, let's define them and look at some specifics.

What are Bid Sites?

A bid site is a place where buyers gather in an attempt to find the perfect freelancer for their project. These sites aren't just limited to writing gigs, but run the gamut. You can find job postings for IT work, social media tasks, marketing, and more. But there are a great many freelance writing projects there.

A buyer will post the details of the project they want to hire a freelancer for, and ask qualified freelancers to bid on the job. Then the posting goes public, which means all active freelancers on that site can view it, and if they want, place a bid on it. (Some jobs are posted as fixed fee jobs, which means the buyer has already set a price for the job instead of accepting bids.)

How to Market Your Empire on a Bid Site

There are two aspects to placing a bid: the marketing of your company and the mechanics of your bid. Here, we'll concentrate on the marketing aspect, and then in a later chapter, I'll give you a step-by-step guide to placing a winning bid.

Bid sites allow three direct opportunities to aggressively market your services. You can do this with the bid itself, your provider page on the bid site, and your client ratings that are attached to each project. At first glance, each of these areas seem to be just a mechanical step in the bid process, and fortunately for you, most of your competitors will view them exactly as that. Oh, but they're so much more.

Come on, let me show you a few secrets of the trade.

Market Yourself as You Place Bids

When you make your first appearance on a bid site, think of it as your personality entering a room. You will be entering a "world" where many players and characters already exist and they are involved in a story line that's in progress. You—the new guy— want to make sure your first impression is memorable. This is where your careful planning in your brand will begin to pay off. Will you come in as the new writer who will do any job for a low, but fair price? As an expert in a difficult field? As an aggressive business owner who won't stop until each of your clients are 100 percent satisfied? However you decide to arrive on the scene, make sure you're the one who controls that all important first impression.

How do you do that? With the words and phrases you use in your bid. Play along with me here and imagine that you are the owner of Crank 'Em Out Writing Services. Your brand promotes a mid-range price with a fast turnaround, made possible by a qualified team of hip, motivated writers. You're fun, efficient, and will always stand behind your work.

It's time to place your first bid. You've nailed down your brand, studied the marketing techniques, and you understand how to write for the market.

Now you've found a project you want to do and you're itching to submit a bid.

Wait.

The next words you type will either bring in business or be completely ignored. Look at the following two examples from our imaginary Empire, and tell me, which company would you hire?

Bid Number One

Hello,

We are a new writing company and are excited about this project. We have a great interest in container gardening, so we feel like we could produce quality articles for you. Our bid is $25 per article, or for the entire 10 articles you are requesting, $250.00.

We look forward to hearing from you,

Crank 'Em Out Writing Services

Y...a...w....n.... Oh, sorry, I dozed off for a moment. Okay, let's look at bid number two.

Bid Number Two

Good morning,

We were so excited to find your project for articles about container gardening. We are avid gardeners, so this subject is not only near and dear to our hearts, but we are also experts on the topic.

We are a team of motivated writers who are known for doing whatever it takes to make our customers happy. In other words, your satisfaction is our number one goal.

> Our bid is $25 per article, for a total of $250 for your entire project of 10 articles. We guarantee a quick turnaround time, expertly written articles, and guaranteed satisfaction in our work.
>
> We would love to add you to our growing list of happy customers!
>
> The team at Crank 'Em Out Writing Services

Do you see the difference? Bid number one exudes no confidence and gives the buyer no real reason to award them the bid. Sure, they sound like a nice group, but hey, when is the last time you bought something because the salesperson was *nice*?

On the other hand, bid number two makes you sit up and take notice. It exudes confidence and a boldness that's difficult to argue with. They talk about their expertise and tell the potential customer exactly what they can expect from their services.

When someone hires a writer, they're earnestly seeking someone who will take their precious project and do it justice. Any buyer reading bid number two would feel confident about putting their project in the capable hands of that writing company.

So, what are the marketing aspects that you should include in all of your bids? (Remember, we'll talk about the mechanics of the bid in a later chapter.) They are:

- Your brand. Make your brand known and stay consistent.

- Confidence. There's a difference between being confident and cocky. A cocky bid will be passed over faster than you can blink, but a confident one is difficult to ignore.

- Your guarantee. The buyer has to be assured that you will stand behind your work. He also wants to be convinced that he will walk away with a viable product.

- Personable. No one wants to do business with an entity, even if you've branded yourself as a company. Make yourself (your personality, your enthusiasm and confidence) jump off the page.

By including all of these elements in your bid in an attention getting way, you will present a complete package to the buyer—not just a bid. The good news? You'll be one of the few who do it. Go ahead, take a look at a few of the bid sites now and see if I'm not telling you the truth.

The Bid Site Portfolio

Your bid site portfolio is different from, and in addition to, your online portfolio (which will talk about in a minute). Most bid sites will provide you with a dedicated page so you can display samples of your work, present a history of your accomplishments, and highlight your areas of expertise.

You can probably guess what I'm about to say, but I'll say it anyway. Don't be like most of your competitors and simply post samples of your work on this important page. Instead, tell a story. Make potential buyers want to stay a while. Remember, the longer they stay and look at your page, the more they'll get to know you. And the more they know you, the more they'll want to do business with you. Here are the best ways to accomplish this.

- **Organize your samples into categories**. Some freelancers put up a hodgepodge of samples and expect buyers to wade through them to find relevant samples for the type of job they want done. That's not putting the client first. Instead, make it easy for them by arranging your samples in categories. For example, your samples could be arranged in category titles like "internet articles," "blogs," "e-books," "sales letters," and "white papers." (Don't worry, we'll specifically address how to write each of these a little later.) This allows buyers a stress free and convenient way to check out your work. The freelancers who don't take this simple step risk losing potential jobs because buyers get too frustrated when trying to find the right samples.

- **Post your best work.** This one should be obvious, but some writers simply put up their latest work, even if it's not the best. If you don't yet have samples, you'll need to create some. Do not attempt to place a bid without samples—no one in their right mind would hire a writer until they've seen samples of their writing style.

- **Post a mix of work.** Not every client is looking for the same type of writing, so it's best to post a mixture of writing styles. For example, you should have samples of light, conversational writing, academic writing, sales copy, and any other style you have available.

- **Answer questions.** Some bid sites will ask you "interview" type questions that you have the option of answering, and if you do, those answers will be posted on your page. You should answer every one of them, but be sure to use them as a way to tell potential buyers your story. Insert as much of your brand as you can. What do I mean? If one of the questions asks what you specialize in, use it to brand yourself in the eyes of buyers.

  For example, a writer who doesn't understand the importance of branding might answer the question like this: "General writer with emphasis on business, automotive and golf."

  Wow—that makes you want to drop everything and hire him on the spot, doesn't it? That same writer could have created a lot more energy and excitement by saying something like this: "Although I do have a few areas of expertise, such as business, automotive, and golf, I love nothing more than the opportunity to take on a project that stretches me. Part of the reason I write for a living is my compulsive love of researching a topic and then writing about it. Just ask my clients—I'm the go-to guy when you need an article about the most obscure topic. My promise to you is that no matter what assignment you give me, whether it be the mating habits of honeybees or lawn mowing 101, it will be well researched and unique.

See the difference? So will the buyers who read your portfolio. And don't forget that you'll be able to link to your own online portfolio from the bid site's page, so you can continue to tell your story there.

Market Your Empire With Ratings

If you've never worked on a bid site before, let me catch you up to speed. On some sites, every bid you place and every project you complete can be seen by everyone—both competitors and potential clients. Your personal online portfolio will be available to everyone. But most importantly, your ratings, both those that you leave for clients, and those left for you by clients, will be in full view of everyone who views your profile.

What are ratings on a bid site, you ask? Everyone who does business on the site will have a place where they can be rated. Writers and every other freelancer are rated by their buyers, and the buyers are rated by the freelancers. The ratings appear at the completion of every job you complete. As you can image, these ratings can make or break a writer. We'll talk later about how to navigate the rating system, but for now, let's concentrate on how it can be used as a marketing tool.

When a buyer is considering your bid, the first thing they'll do is check the ratings left by other buyers. Now, you can't control what the buyers say about you, other than making sure that you always meet your deadlines with well researched and polish work. This is critical. A writer who has unfavorable ratings on a bid site may as well unplug their computer. Let me put it this way, if a buyer is deciding between two writers and one has all favorable ratings and the other has a few that are not so good, which one do you think the buyer will hire?

But you don't only have to worry about the ratings your clients leave for you. It's a little known fact that many buyers also check the ratings you have left for other buyers. After all, this is where your true personality comes out, isn't it?

Imagine that a buyer was so impressed with the sample site portfolio you set up. He was impressed with your can-do attitude and willingness to tackle difficult jobs. He clicked through to your online portfolio and was pleased to see the continuing theme of the go-to guy who loves to tackle challenging projects. He felt sure he'd finally found the writer he was looking for.

Then, just as a last a precaution, he decides to check out the ratings you've left for previous buyers. You know, just to make sure you're a team player. What if this is what he saw?

- **Rating for client A.** I was disappointed in this buyer because he didn't communicate the complexity of the project when he hired me. As a result, it took twice as long to complete it then what I'd budgeted. I would work for him again, but only with a better understanding of the project up front.

- **Rating for client B.** I liked the work, but the buyer was slow to pay. I had to stay on him to get paid.

- **Rating for client C.** This guy is never satisfied. Geez, I felt like I couldn't do anything right.

Can't you just see the buyer back pedaling now? Rapidly? It's vital to remember that your buyer feedback is an extension of your brand. To quote moms across the globe, if you don't have anything nice to say, then don't say anything at all.

Now I can hear some of you thinking that the ratings seemed to make valid points. It appears so, but let me ask you a question. When is the last time you saw any legitimate business airing its client's dirty laundry for all the world to see?

What it comes down to is this: do you want to build an Empire or would you rather have the fleeting satisfaction of vindication? You decide.

The Online Portfolio

Imagine a travel agency without colorful brochures showing the destinations they offer. What about Avon without its catalogs? An online jewelry store without photos of its products? In short, if any of these businesses tried to operate without the essential marketing tools, they wouldn't survive very long. And in today's market, neither will a writer without a web portfolio.

Anyone can talk a good game, but in the business atmosphere that today's writers operate in, you'd better be able to back up that talk if you want to land any projects.

What's an online portfolio? It's your own website that is designed to showcase your work. It doesn't have to be extravagant or costly, but it does have to be unique, thoroughly branded, and relevant. We've already discussed the mechanical aspects of your online portfolio, so now let's look at how you can use it to market your Empire.

Having read this far, you already understand that your portfolio must be branded through and through. If a client is considering you for a project on a bid site, it will most likely be their third interaction with you and your company. They've read your bid, gone to the bid sites portfolio, and now they have clicked through to your online portfolio. Now is the time to present the full scope of your abilities, and make it clear to the client why you are the best person for the job.

Obviously, you'll need to display a full range of writing samples, everything from short articles to more complex projects such as special reports, white papers, and e-books. These should be arranged in a format that makes it easy for the buyer to navigate your site. For instance, if this particular buyer is considering hiring you for a serious of articles about running a small business, he should be able to find your business content easily. It should be grouped together and identified as such.

But other than presenting a branded professional site filled with genius inspired writing, how else can you use your website to market your services? Here are a few suggestions.

- **Use client testimonials.** In your online interactions with buyers, you will frequently receive compliments and praise for your work. Save them and post them on your site.

- **Make it easy to work with you.** Include announcements about rush jobs, packaged deals, and retainer jobs. Get creative with how you sell your content.

- **Offer referral fees.** Pay clients a small fee (or credit toward their next purchase) for any new projects you receive as a result of their referrals.

- **Link often**. Make sure to link your online portfolio to every site where a buyer may be looking. The possibilities are literally endless. For example, if you're a writer who specializes in interior design, join every interior design forum you can find and include your website link in your signature line. When you post comments, anyone who reads them will see the link, and that could lead to business. Remember, it's considered rude to blatantly market yourself on these forums, but having a link in your signature line is perfectly acceptable.

- **Exchange links.** There are numerous ways you can link your site to other sites by mutual agreement. For example, let's use the above example of a writer who specializes in interior design. The writer may agree to display links for home accessories or furniture on his site in exchange for that site displaying links to his site with a tag line that says "Writer specializing in interior design."

- **Write informative articles**. By including a few articles on your website that appeal directly to your buyer's needs, you'll establish yourself as a helpful expert. And in addition to pulling in potential clients from search engines, these articles will show buyers that you have their best interests at heart. For example, you could write a series of articles directed at website owners listing the best practices when hiring freelance writers, or write an article listing the questions they should always ask a writer before hiring them.

And speaking of using articles to draw people to your website, let me tell you about one of the best ways you can use these articles to bring in new business.

Write Articles for Other Sites

Let me lay out a scenario for you. Imagine that you own a website that sells custom lighting, and you're looking to increase traffic to your site. One of the first things website owners do to accomplish this is to add unique, relevant content to their site. This particular website owner needs a writer, but wants one who can write intelligently about custom lighting.

Our same writer from the previous example has decided to increase his exposure by writing articles for sites that his potential buyers might read. He writes articles for several sites, all of which gladly post them on their blog because they're always looking for relevant, free content. At the end of each article, which are all about different aspects of interior design, his signature tagline says, "John Smith, freelance writer specializing in interior design. You can contact him at hiswebsite.com.

It doesn't take much imagination to figure out what happens when the custom lighting website owner reads an article on one of the industry blogs our writer has posted on. A sale is made, and pretty soon afterwards, more sales as "John Smith" becomes known in that professional circle as the writer to go to for articles about interior design

How to Find Blogs to Write For

If you're going to write articles for other sites, which is called guest blogging, you'll need to find the best sites in your niche. For example, our writer who specializes in interior design would need a list of the sites that accept guest posts from other people who are experts on the topic. Luckily, there are a few simple ways to do this. Here are two of my favorites.

Google Long Tail Keywords

One of the simplest ways to find blogs that are open to guest bloggers is to use a series of long tail keywords to track them down. A long tail keyword is just as it sounds—a keyword consisting of more than one word.

To do this, our interior design writer would certain keywords into Google to look for possible blogs. He would first enter "interior design," then tack on words to narrow down his search. (Be sure to substitute your niche word for "interior design" in the following examples)

Interior design+ guest post blogs
Interior design + guest post sites
Interior design + guest posting sites
Interior design + accept guest posts
Interior design + write for us
Interior design + guest post wanted
Interior design + guest blogger
Interior design + submit guest blog post

Do you see? If you are a small business writer, simply substitute the words "small business" for "interior design." These are just some of the terms you can use to find dozens of sites you can write for.

Or, Do it the Easy Way

If you are looking for an even easier way to find blogs to write for, you can use a site called Alltop.com. Use its search feature to type in your keyword, and you'll be shown a whole slew of blogs that you send a request to about guest blogging for them.

Advertising Your Services

So far, we've talked about the various ways you can call attention to your online portfolio and website for free, and hey, I'm all about free promotions but there's an area of paid marketing that simply cannot be ignored: placing paid advertisements in areas where potential buyers hang out.

For example, our writer who specializes in interior design could place an ad on a website where manufacturers of interior design products gather to discuss the market. The ad, which would advertise his writing service for that industry, could either be placed on that site's blog or on the front page of the site.

In addition to placing ads directly on websites, social media ads are a great way to get the word out about your business. Many people have great luck with Facebook ads. They aren't expensive, and in fact, you can control how much you spend each day on the ads when you set it up. And you'll be able to target the ads to your audience the same way you can when you select a relevant website. For example, our writer could target people interested in interior design and marketing.

The ads won't contain a lot of detail because you'll only have a certain number of characters to catch the attention of those who see them. Questions work well, as do bold statements that are difficult to ignore. Our writer could run an ad that says "Looking for a writer who specializes in interior design topics? Click here to see free samples." If the ad catches a potential buyer's attention, they will be able to click on the link, which would take them to the writer's online portfolio. They can then browse through the writer's entire collection of articles. In other words, they'll have everything they need to make a hiring decision just seconds after they click the ad.

Building a Client List

Oh, the things you can do with a client list. I don't care if you only write one article for someone, or write thousands for a client, never, and I repeat, never throw out any of their contact information. Instead, keep a careful list of their information, including how they found you, what projects you did for them, and any other relevant information you gather on them. Why? Because despite all your skill, despite the fact that you've followed every sales and marketing tip you've ever heard, getting and retaining clients comes down to this: relationship. A buyer is going to do business with the writer he or she likes. Period.

Don't believe me? Then just try to build your Empire without developing relationships with your clients. And then after you've come to your senses, come back and pick up this book. I promise I won't rub it in too much.

So, just what is a client list and how can you use it to build your Empire?

A client list is exactly what it sound like: a list of every client you've ever worked for, along with the pertinent data that makes them a person to you, and not just a client. Ultimately, this will help you in your attempts to get more business from them in the future.

Personally, I use a spreadsheet and every time I have an interaction with a client where I learn something important, I add the details the line dedicated to that client. As soon as you get your first client, you should create your own spreadsheet and then begin compiling the data you collect. You will use this spreadsheet throughout your career to pull in more business. Here are some of the ways you'll use this list.

Start a Newsletter

What do you think the number one reason is for creating and sending out an online newsletter? If you answered that it's to keep your clients informed about what's going on in the industry, you would probably be in the majority.

But let's be honest.

The real reason most business owners take the time to produce a company newsletter is twofold. The first goal is to keep your business name in front of your clients so that when they need a writer, they'll automatically think of you. Secondly, a newsletter will help convince your clients that they need your services again. Now. And if they happen to get a little informed about the goings on in the industry, that's all the better. The tricky part is to cloak your two goals into an informative and helpful newsletter.

There are numerous ways to do this. Let me

illustrate this by giving you an example of a newsletter, and then we'll dissect it together.

The Crank 'Em Out Monthly Newsletter

Headline article:
Now Offering e-book Writing Services

After numerous requests from our clients, we've finally decided to add e-books to the list of services we offer. Our normal fee for a 20 page e-book will be $750, but the first five people to order will receive an introductory price of $500. Click here to see a sample e-book…

Article #2: The Latest Research on Keyword Usage to Help Draw Visitors to Your Site

Here at Crank 'Em Out Writing Services, we stay on top of the latest trends and research in order to produce the most results-oriented content for you. That's why we're excited to tell you about the latest research and how we plan to apply it to your content…

Article #3: Summer Special

It's hot again, and our answer to that is to give you some relief from the heat by offering you a special summer deal. Order $100 or more in articles 500 words or less, and we'll take 10 percent of your entire order!

Article #4: Awe-Shucks

Lucy Moore sent us a special thank you after a job we completed for her, and we thought we'd pass it

---

> along. "Working with Crank 'Em Out Writing Services has been the best freelancer experience I've had in my 20 year career. You've won my business for life!"
> Thanks, Lucy. We think you're pretty special, too.

By now I shouldn't have to say this, but you know I'm going to anyway so let's get it over with: make sure your newsletter is branded, both in content and style. After that, you'll need to make sure every aspect of your newsletter is relevant. In other words, you've got to give them a reason to not hit the delete button.

The best way to do that is to ensure that your headline—the first thing they'll see—is attention grabbing. In our example, the headline announces that the company is adding a new service, e-books. What's more, the lead sentence makes it clear that it was only after numerous clients asked for it that they decided to do it. Many of the clients reading this would instantly wonder what the competition knows that they don't, and it might start them thinking that they need an e-book, too.

Next, an urgent offer is made that only the first five people will get. The reader is invited to click a link that will take them to a page on the online portfolio that displays an e-book sample. Hopefully, that, in combination with the urgency of the offer, will close the deal and put $500 in the writer's pocket.

But what if the client doesn't want an e-book? Well, certainly every client has an interest in keyword rich internet content, the very thing that drives all those visitors to their websites. That's why the newsletter contains a second sale—one that will appeal to every reader because it offers a discount on the products they already buy.

The next article is included to boost the writer's reputation as an expert. And even if the readers don't want to know the technical aspects of what makes a keyword article work in Google's algorithm, they will be happy to know that the writer understands it and is concerned about keeping up with the trends. After all, his services are what they rely on to build their site's business.

Finally, just to make sure the clients understand that they're working with the best, a client testimonial reiterates what a wonderful service the writer offers. This adds credence to your claims, and makes it fun to spotlight a new client every time a new newsletter is released.

An online newsletter is a proven marketing tool. And if it's done right, it will become a good source of new and repeat business. Now, let's take a look at another effective tool you should utilize.

Special Email Announcements

Any time you have timely, noteworthy news such as a new product, an improved way of doing things, or are offering a sale or discount, your clients will probably want to know. One way to do this is with an email making the special announcement, and they can take one of two forms. The form you choose will depend on how personal you are with your clients. Let's call them the personal and impersonal approach. Here are the differences.

The Impersonal Email Announcement

Let's use our friends at Crank 'Em Out Writing Services. They've just added e-books to their repertoire of services and they want their current clients to be the first to know. They have branded their Empire as a business entity, and so they decide to create a general type of announcement that can be sent to their entire list of clients. It might look something like this:

> Crank 'Em Out Writing Service Now Offers e-books!
>
> We thought you'd want to be among the first to know that we've added e-books to our list of services. Click here to see a sample of our work. To kick things off, we are offering the first five books at $250 off our regular price of $750. Click here to send us an email claiming yours.

As you know, depending on the mood of your recipients, some of your announcements may be deleted or ignored. But by making sure the subject line is solid, you will grab the attention of those buyers who are considering the product.

Now let's look at how to make the announcement more up close and personal.

Personal Email Announcement

If you've branded yourself as a friendly writer who maintains an easy, casual communication style with your clients, then you will be in a position to truly personalize your email announcements. How? By simply sending your clients an e-mail telling them what you're doing. Sound too easy? Put yourself in the shoes of a busy website owner who has to weed through dozens of emails a day. As you're reviewing them, you come across one that looks like this from a writer you've used in the past:

Subject line: New Project?

Now, you used this writer before, but don't remember if you've assigned him any new projects so you open the e-mail just in case. Here is what you find:

> Hello Mrs. Client,
> I hope all is well with you. I just thought you would like to know that I'm now providing e-books for my clients. A lot of clients have asked me for them since they're so popular right now, and I'm excited to tell you that I'm now taking orders for them. To celebrate this milestone, we're offering a half price discount on the first 5 e-books ordered. If you want to know more, I've written an article on how they can be used to market your business. To see it, click here.
> I hope to talk to you soon. Have a wonderful day.
> The team at Crank 'Em Out Writing Services

Of course the link would take the client to the promised article, which is located on your online portfolio. They will also find all the details about your e-book offerings. Pretty slick, huh?

Finally as you communicate with your clients,

you'll come to know things like their birthday, when they move, or have children. These occasions, as well as national holidays such as Easter and Christmas, are excellent times to send a properly branded E card. It will serve as a reminder that you're still there, waiting patiently for your next assignment.

Okay, now that you're up to speed on how to bring in business, let's talk about what you'll be writing.

Empire Builders Arch Enemy #4:
Not Understanding Different Buyer Types

It's a mistake to tailor all of your marketing efforts to the same type of buyer. In general, there are three types of buyers, and each one is looking for different things from you. They are:

- The Price Focused Buyer. These people are price conscious and will generally go with the low bidder.

- The Relationship Focused Buyer: This type of buyer wants to build a relationship with a writer and use them for all his needs.

- The Quality Focused Buyer: This buyer is looking for a writer who will provide top quality and will generally pay whatever it takes to get it.

CHAPTER 6:

Empire Basics— What to Write and How to Do It

It's time to move on to the practicalities of building your Empire. The types of content that buyers will hire you to write is literally limitless, but there are some project types that you will see over and over again. Let's take a look at some of them.

Keyword Articles

The keyword article is to the Internet what gasoline is to a car. It's what drives and directs the millions of users to the websites they're searching for. Have you ever wondered how, when you type in the words "cocker spaniel breeders" into a search engine, the results that show up are magically what you'd hoped for?

The sites that show up high on the results pages do so because they have strategically used keywords in their website articles. What is a keyword? It's a carefully selected word or phrase that website owners think people will use when looking for their product or service. There is an art to selecting the effective keywords, but as a writer you won't need to provide them. The client will tell you which keywords to include in the articles.

For example, if a site owner offered cocker spaniel breeding services, he would use keywords related to his services in the articles on his site. He might use cocker spaniel, cocker spaniels, cocker spaniel breeder, and cocker spaniel breeders. In other words, in order for a website to be found, its content must include the keywords people are most likely to type into a search engine when doing a search for a particular product or information.

Website owners love to hire writers who understand how to write keyword articles, but it's not as easy as it sounds. Each client has their own interpretation about where and how many times a keyword should appear in an article. And it's the writer's job to follow those specifications, and at the same time create an informative article that doesn't sound choppy or unnatural.

That's not always easy to do when the client insist on including awkward keywords or too many keywords in an article. For example, if a local website wants to be found, the keyword articles need to include the name of the city it's located in. This is called local SEO (search engine optimization). So your client may give you keywords that look like this: Las Vegas cocker spaniel breeding services. Or even worse, you may be asked to write an article with a keyword like this: cocker spaniel breeding services Las Vegas.

The trick is to place the keywords in the articles in a way that sounds natural. For example, you could place the last keyword in the article like this: Are you looking for Cocker Spaniel breeding services? Las Vegas has one you should know about.

Log onto to any website and study the content they have. You'll soon begin to see a pattern with the keywords used in the articles. Study them, and write a few on your own for practice if you've never done it before.

The E-book

You are currently reading an e-book. Now before you accuse me of stating the excruciatingly obvious, let me make a point. There is a huge misconception that e-books don't have to measure up to traditionally printed books. But the truth is that if someone is going to take the time to read a book, whether it's a print book or an e-book, it needs to meet certain standards or the reader will walk away unsatisfied. In other words, if you're given an assignment to write an e-book, it should be handled as professionally as you would treat a traditionally printed book.

Now, let me get back to my point. The e-book you are reading now was born from a deep desire to help struggling freelance writers make a full-time living doing what they love. Untold hours of thought, planning, research, and writing went into this book, and I've made it the best that I believe it can be.

But what if my attitude had been that since I was only producing an e-book, I didn't really have to put that much work into it? That as long as I had an eye-catching cover and description, buyers would purchase it anyway?

Let me ask you, the buyer, how you would feel about that? I thought so. As a fellow writer, I urge you to remember this: the e-book market will only be viable as long as the consumer can expect a good product.

Having said that, be aware that there are writers out there who will write an entire e-book for $100. These are generally new writers who don't quite understand the amount of time they'll have to dedicate to it. And to their credit, they will usually only make that mistake once. But unfortunately, there are buyers who also don't understand what goes into producing a quality e-book, and my advice to you is to only work with those who do—and are willing to pay you a professional fee for good quality work.

Just like any other type of book, there are certain things every client will expect. For example, you should always include a table of contents. Some buyers will submit a table of contents to you and ask you to follow it as you write the book. Others will expect you to create your own. Some will trust your judgment while others will ask to approve it before you begin the work. All of these are acceptable. If you are asked to create the table of contents, be sure you put a lot of thought and planning into it. Please see the table of contents at the front of this book as an example.

An e-book can range from 25 pages to 500, and there are no absolutes. Currently, the preferred style is a shorter book of about 100 pages that are filled with actionable and informative content. Before giving a buyer a bid, be sure you understand his length requirements.

Included in the body of most e-books are the following:

Links. One of the greatest things about e-books is that they can be designed to be used interactively. For example, adding a link to enhance the readers understanding or experience goes a long way towards their satisfaction with a book. When including links in a client's e-book, be sure to get them approved.

Photos. Some buyers will ask you to include photos in their e-book. Sometimes the client will provide you with them, while others want you to search them out on your own. If you are required to locate the photos, you can find them at sites like Shutterstock, and FreeDigitalPhotos. Simply insert the URL for the photo and the client will buy them and insert them after you've submitted the book. Be sure that you negotiate this properly with the client before taking on the job so you're not stuck having to pay for the photos.

Blog Posts

It makes sense for website owners to attach a blog to their site because it's a great way to draw visitors who are looking for information related to the products or services they sell. Remember, when keywords are strategically placed in articles or blogs, it helps bring visitors to a site.

A well-designed blog can be a thing of beauty, and setting up a blog to attract traffic to a website is one of the best ways to get new customers.

Most website owners know this, but don't have the time or ability to write the blogs themselves. What's more, not just anyone can write blog posts that will keep people checking in at the site for more. Remember our lessons on branding? A blog is part of a business' brand.

The fact that blogs are so important to the success of a website is why so many site owners hire freelance writers to write their blogs for them. And if you land a gig like this, your ability to create a following is what will make you a success. The first thing you'll need to do is have a discussion with the buyer to determine what type of style he is looking for. Here are some examples of blog styles.

- **Controversial.** In this type of blog, it will be your job to stir up the masses and get a heated debate going. A good controversial blogger will understand the line between arguing and a healthy debate, and have the ability to maintain it. For example, a controversial blog could be a political blog where the writer takes the minority opinion.

- **Informative.** In this type of blog, the blogger keeps his readers informed about issues that matter to them. A fitness or healthy eating blog are good examples.

- **Humorous.** Many people appreciate humor, and if a blogger can create an atmosphere that makes readers laugh, he will likely develop a huge following.

- **Activist.** This type of blog is written to spur the reader to action. A prolife blogger who uses this medium to schedule rallies and talk about his cause is a perfect example.

Finally here are some things you should know about writing blogs for clients. You probably won't receive a byline when you are writing blogs for your clients. Most likely, the client will attach his own name to your writing. This is called ghost blogging.

In addition, your client will dictate the number of times per week that you post a blog. This typically ranges from one to five times per week.

The blog posts that typically get the most attention are lists and how to posts. Remember that list of relevant niche blogs you looked for earlier? Visit a few of them and pay attention to how they format them and what they write about to give you some ideas on how to best approach a blog post.

White Papers

Sometimes a website owner will want to put together a special report to either give away or sell on their website. This is called a white paper, and it is typically an in-depth report that contains pertinent facts and information about a specific topic. For instance, the owner of a website that lists used cars for sale may decide to put together a white paper giving readers the essential information they need to properly by a used car. This report would be jam packed with useful ideas and tips that would help the car buyer make a better decision.

A white paper is not as long as an e-book, but it is typically longer than an Internet article. The length will depend on the buyer's wishes, but they tend to run between 2000 and 3000 words. In traditional print, it might be called a booklet.

If you have been hired to write a white paper, know that your standards should be very high. The buyers of these products typically pay well and will expect to get their money's worth.

Sales Letters

Almost everyone on the Internet is trying to sell something, and many of them use sales letters to do that. If you've ever happened upon a site with a long letter telling you the benefits of a product, you've seen a sales letter. It's a tool that many website owners use, and if it's written correctly, it will increase a site's sales.

Sales letters are typically written in a personable manner, and tend to speak one-on-one to the reader. But even though they appear effortless and breezy, most follow a standard format. The sales letter has one goal: to sell a product.

Many buyers will insist on only hiring proven sales letter writers, while others are willing to take a chance on a less experienced writer. Needless to say, a writer who has proven his ability to generate sales can demand much higher fees than the beginning writer. Let's take a look at the basic formula and discuss what makes a sales letter work.

- **The Headline.** This is also called the deck copy, and it should instantly grab the reader's attention with a bold claim or (almost) unbelievable fact.

- **The Introduction**. Also called a lead, this is where expert writers tap into the emotions of readers to make them want to continue reading. For instance, you could make them feel guilty, scared, hopeful, prideful or angry about something to get them to continue to read.

- **The Body.** This is the longest part of a sales letter, and in it, the writer should methodically take the reader through these things: setting them up for the sale, telling them why the solution or product is so special and why it's better than the competition, why the person selling it is the expert on the matter, the benefits of the product or service, and finally, showing the reader others who have used it and benefited from it.

- **The Offer**. This is the part of the sales letter that makes people push the buy button. The theory is that you are giving them X number of dollars when they spend X number of dollars. For example, "If you buy this product for $49, I'll throw in $29 worth of X and another $20 worth of Y." This typically works to close a sale, which is why you see so many people "throwing in" more items when they're trying to sell you something. Do this part right, and you'll create a sales letter that sells for your client.

Website Copy

Finally, many buyers hire freelance writers to write the copy for their website pages. Buyers may hire you write their home page copy, or any other pages such as the About Us page, Contact Us page, or the specialty pages on their site.

The key to writing effective website copy is to understand the goal of the page you're writing and move the reader towards that goal. For example, if the goal of the home page is to get people to click to the products page, then you might spend some time telling them about the benefits of the products they'll find there.

Be sure to understand the client's brand before you begin writing so your copy will resonate with the intended users.

In the end, every project you're hired to do will revolve around creating content that is personable, informative, and well-researched. You're sure to come across other types of projects, but this is a list of the most common ones you'll encounter.

Where to Find Work

Now that you know what you will be writing, you should know where to find the buyers that will hire you. You will get most of your work from bid sites and other writing job boards. Here is a list of some of the best places to find work:

ProBlogger. The buyers on this site are specifically looking for writers to do blogging jobs.

Online Writing Jobs. This is one of my favorite sites because it always has a wide of variety of interesting jobs that will appeal to every writer.

Outsource.com. You can find jobs on this site, or use it to post a help wanted ad when you need to hire a writer.

Freelancer.com. This is a great site for both finding freelance writers to work for you, or to post help wanted listings yourself.

UpWork.com. This site merged with ODesk and Elance to make a huge site that has hundreds of job postings waiting for you to bid on them. You can also list your own help wanted postings on this site.

Guru.com. This was one of the first bid sites on the scene, and it's still going strong with 1.5 million freelancers registered and looking for jobs. You'll be able to bid on projects on this site, or when you're ready, hire writers.

SimplyHired.com. This is another site that lists jobs nationwide. Simply use keywords like "writer" or "blogger" to find the jobs that are right for you.

Freelancejobopenings.com. This site is great for looking for jobs, as well as finding writers when you're ready to hire one.

LinkedIn. Some people use search terms on LinkedIn to find freelance writers, so as you get some jobs under your belt, it's smart to have a profile with the title Freelance Writing Business. I can't tell you how many jobs I've received this way.

Morning Coffee Newsletter. Sign up for this weekly newsletter and receive a truckload of jobs in your inbox every day.

FreelanceWritingGigs.com. This site updates their list daily with new job postings for writers and bloggers.

One you've completed a few jobs and are ready to move up to higher paying jobs, you will have to expand your search. (Although the sites listed above do offer some higher paying jobs). MakeaLiving.com offers a comprehensive list of places that pay $50 or more per article, with some paying a few hundred dollars. Keep in mind that you shouldn't start out with these sites, but plan to work your way up to them as your skills improve.

Empire Builders Arch Enemy #5: Not Practicing Writing Before Bidding on Jobs

Reading about a keyword article or sales letter is one thing, but actually doing it is quite another. Before you begin to place bids, you should take some time to write samples for each of the project types I've covered. (You'll need them for your portfolio, anyway.) Don't wait until you receive a project to learn the art of writing these types of content. Doing so could result in bad ratings or unsatisfied clients—both of which will negatively impact your Empire.

CHAPTER 7:

Launch Your Empire: YOU are the Foundation

Whew! That was a lot of work just to get to the place where we can officially talk about launching your Empire. So by now, you've branded your business, you've familiarized yourself with the various bid sites, you've checked out the competition, and you've written sample pieces and used them to build your online portfolio. If you have truly put your best effort into all of the above, smile. You've just built an unshakable foundation for your very own Empire.

You'll spend the first month strengthening the foundation step-by-step all by yourself. Why? Because it's important that you learn the business—every aspect of it. I don't care how long you've been writing, I guarantee that you don't know the business like I outline it in this book. By flying solo for the first month, you'll quickly learn everything there is to know about your Empire. You will have walked in your writer's shoes, and have a firm grasp on what can and can't be done. You'll know what works and what doesn't, and have a concrete idea of how long things take.

But I warn you—it's not going to be easy. But then again, nothing ever is that's worth something, is it?

What I'd like to do first is show you an outline of your activities for the first day, week, and month. Are you ready? Let's get building.

Day One

It's your first day as the owner of your Empire. Are you ready to rule? The first order of business is getting some clients, and that's what you will be doing all day. Since you've already familiarized yourself with the various job bid sites, you should be able to immediately begin placing bids. I will give you a step-by-step guide for placing bids later in this chapter.

The first thing you'll realize is how time consuming this process is. There are literally thousands of project offerings out there, and in order to make the best use of your time and ensure that you get the jobs you'll be the most successful at, it's necessary that you begin your search by category.

Every writer has areas that their most comfortable with, and that's where you should start. Remember, the first quarter you will be working alone, and so by accepting jobs that you already have some knowledge about, you will be much more able to meet your goals.

So imagine that your areas of expertise lies in small business and family issues. I highly recommend that the first day be spent bidding on every job in those categories on all the bid sites. Why all of them, you ask? Because thus far you don't have a reputation built up, so it's necessary that you cast a wide net.

It's also important to take note of the deadlines that are attached to each of the projects. Someone may want 20 articles in two days, and another buyer may want 10 articles in a day. Individually these would both be difficult, but doable, but together they would be impossible for one person. You won't need to worry about this when you place your bids because you won't win every project you bid on. In the case that you do win too many projects, you can negotiate time lines with the buyers.

So, to sum up your first day, it should look something like this:

8:00 AM to 5:00 PM. Place a bid for every project in your categories of expertise on every bidding site. For your first day you should pick two broad categories. For example, most people can write intelligently about home finances, credit, pets, or any other general topic with a minimum amount of research.

At the end of your first day, you may even have your very first job. Congratulations! You are well on your way to building your writing Empire.

Your First Week

If you followed my advice for the first day, you laid a critical foundation for your first quarter. In fact, as you sit down at your computer the next morning, you'll likely have some inquiries from prospective clients, and maybe even a job or two.

But now it's a new day, so let's see what else there is to be done. The first order of the day is to immediately answer any prospective client inquiries.

When working online, it's imperative that your communications with clients be swift. They will expect no less from an internet writer.

Some of the buyers may request to see more writing samples, some may have a question about your fee, or some may attempt to negotiate a better fee. Handle them all quickly and professionally.

Next, accept any job offers you received. You will have to officially accept them through the bid site. Be sure to pay attention to all the deadlines and make sure you can meet them. If not, be honest with the clients and ask for an extension because of a conflicting project. Be sure to do this before you accept the job. Most clients prefer a busy writer who is honest about their schedule over one who promises something they can't deliver.

Next, you'll need to follow up on all bids placed the day before. Why, you ask? Because it's one of the most important things you can do to bring in the business. Let me illustrate the importance of this step by showing you a snapshot of Charlie Clients morning.

Charlie Client's day started as it usually did, with dozens of emails and orders for the organic gardening products he sells on his website. He gulps his hot coffee and sets about the task of filling orders and answering questions from people who have visited his site.

About a quarter of the way through his emails, he comes across an e-mail from the bid site where he placed an ad for a writer the day before. He clicks it open and groans. He's received 97 bids on the project. How will he ever find the time to sort and screen these writers? He closes the e-mail, planning to go through the bids once he finishes the work on his desk.

But a few emails later, he sees another e-mail from the bid site. He opens it to find that one of the writers who bid on his project sent him a follow up e-mail. It reads:

> Dear Mr. Charlie Client,
> I placed a bid yesterday for your organic gardening project, and it's been on my mind since I first saw it. I would truly love to work on this project. Please feel free to contact me with any questions, and meanwhile, I've attached a few more samples of my work for your convenience.
> Best to you,
> One smart writer

Curious, Charlie Client reads through the sample articles and is pleased to find that a couple are even related to his intended topic, organic gardening. The articles are well-written and informative. Charlie Client checks the bid price and is happy to find that it is within his budget. He thinks back to the other 96 bids waiting for him to evaluate, most of which he knows won't be qualified, and looks again at this writer's e-mail. Charlie Client smiles and clicks to the bid site to award the writer the bid. He is relieved when he sees the dozens of emails that contain bids from the other writers. He's just saved himself a lot of time, which is something he always needs more of.

Do you see my point? Trust me, by doing this one extra step, you'll advance your Empire exponentially.

Next, you'll want to go to your specified

categories on the bid sites and look for any new job postings. If you find some, place a bid for them. Be sure to keep track of the new bids so that the next morning you will know which ones to send a follow up note to.

Finally, spend the rest of that day writing articles for your newly acquired projects. At this point you should be able to produce 3-4 articles a day, unless you already have some experience. So, the days in your first week should look something like this:

8:00 AM to 8:30 AM. Answer client inquiries and accept jobs.

8:30 AM to 9:30 AM. Send follow up emails for bids placed the day before.

9:30 AM to 10:30 AM. Place bids on the new jobs posted.

10:30 AM to noon. Begin conducting research for the articles you will write that day.

Noon to 1:00 PM. Lunch. It's important to step away from the computer for a lunch break when you work from home. This will help you to stay motivated throughout the day.

1:00 PM to 5:00 PM. Write your articles for the day. Hopefully, you will be able to write at least three articles on your first day. To accomplish this, you may have to work past 5:00 PM.

Obviously, this exact schedule will not work for everyone, so you'll have to figure out what works best for you. And depending on the amount of projects you were awarded, you may have to spend more time writing. Please be aware that no matter how busy you get, you cannot skip the first four steps. If you do, you'll find yourself in a feast or famine cycle. In other words, you'll stay busy for a week and then once you've completed all of your projects, you'll have to start over with bidding for more. That's called mere survival and it's no way to build an Empire.

Having said that, let me make one more point: Rome wasn't built in a day. In fact it took many years and a whole lot of help. My point is that you will have to invest lots of time and energy into your Empire to make it a success. You may find yourself working long days or even over the weekend in order to meet your deadlines. I've done it, and anyone who tells you that you can achieve success with only a minimal amount of effort is lying to you.

After all, you're not punching a clock, you're building an Empire.

At the end of your first week, you should be getting into a steady, productive rhythm. You've likely worked out the kinks in your bidding process, have gotten faster at producing articles, and are feeling more confident. In addition, you should have a feel for your working pace by now, and know which topics you can work faster at and which ones you'll need to dedicate more time to.

Since you'll undoubtedly have more articles to write, hopefully you streamlined the bidding process as you've become more familiar with it. As a general rule, you should be writing about 7 articles a day now, and at 45 minutes each, that accounts for a little over 5 hours per day. Your hours have likely increased and will continue doing so until you make your first hire. Hang on, you're almost there.

Now let's take a look at your first month.

Your First Month

By now you're a well-oiled writing machine. You're sending out bids for jobs not only related to your specialty areas, but you've managed to branch out a little. You've earned some loyal customers who are giving you repeat business because you always meet your deadlines with well-researched, nicely written copy. No doubt about it, you're on a roll. You may even be thinking that the money you paid for this book was the best money you ever spent.

I have something to tell you. The next three months will be the most hectic, difficult, and exhausting months of the building process. But they are vital to the foundation of your Empire. And remember, without a proper foundation, your Empire will surely crumble. Please don't try and take shortcuts here.

I've been there and I know the temptations. You're probably thinking that there's no reason why you can't hire writers right now to help handle all of the work, right? Wrong. You haven't yet built a stable enough foundation to truly support them. Or, you're wondering if you really need to place bids every day. It would be a huge mistake not to. If you don't, you won't be ready to hire your first employee at the designated time, and you'll have to start building your foundation all over again. And if you do that, there is no way you'll meet your yearly goal.

For the next three months, you should strive to write 10 articles a day plus attend to the logistics of your business. That includes communicating with your clients, accepting bids, and bidding on new work in order to fuel your growth. As you can guess, you will work more than 8 hours a day during this time.

I know, it's going to be nearly impossible. But that's what separates you from the surfs. You've got what it takes, right? You're so close. Ready for a little motivation? Let's look at your potential earnings for this period.

If you write seven articles per day the first week and 10 articles a day the next three weeks, you will have written 185 articles your first full month. If you are paid $25.00 per article, your earnings will be $4,625. If you continue to write 10 articles a day for the next two months, you will have written a total of 585 articles, and at $25 each, you will bank $14,625. (You'll need that soon for your Empire, so don't spend it all in one place.) But for now, go and grab yourself an ice cream cone or something because you certainly deserve it.

As you've probably figured out, if you were to continue working at this breakneck speed for the rest of the year, the most you could possibly earn is $60,000. That's not a bad income, but the goal here is to earn a great living without killing yourself in the process. That's why the key to building your foundation is hiring other writers. But before we talk about that, I want to address three areas that you're bound to be wondering about.

What if You're Not Winning Bids?

If you've gone a week without winning any bids, it's time to review and change your approach. Specifically, you'll need to look closely at three areas: the wording in your bids, your pricing, and your portfolio. In order to be a successful bidder, each of these areas must be in complete harmony. Your pricing must reflect your writing skill, which is displayed in your portfolio. Your bid must have the same brand as your portfolio, and it must exude enough confidence to justify your price.

For a review of how to write a bid letter, brand yourself, communicate with clients, or set your pricing, go back to the last chapter. Remember finding the perfect harmony and branding for your Empire may take some effort, but once accomplished, you will hold in your hands the keys to your Empire.

How to Avoid Client Scams

One thing you'll surely run into after placing bids is a client inquiry requesting that you communicate and do business with them off the bid site. My advice to you is to run from these types of clients. There is no legitimate reason to do business off-site. Those fees you pay are well worth it. They protect you from clients who would accept your work and then refuse to pay you for it. Many unscrupulous clients have lured naïve writers off site with the promise of a big project, and once the writers do the work for them, they disappear without paying for the work. Over time you will build relationships with clients and work with them away from bid sites, but in the beginning, I recommend that you use the sites until you learn the ins and outs of this business.

The Anatomy of a Bid

We've spent a lot of time talking about bids, so I think it's about time we took one apart and analyzed it. Let's go through the bidding process step-by-step so there won't be any confusion. I'll start with a typical project posting on one of the bid sites. As you've probably already discovered in your research, a typical project posting looks something like this:

I need 20 articles about organic gardening
Pay rate: between $15.00 and $30.00 per article
Deadline: two weeks
Description: I need an expert writer to create 20 articles on various topics about organic gardening. You will submit the list of topics for our approval.

The first thing you'll notice about a job posting is the subject line. Typically, it will be short and sweet, and with those few words you should be able to get a good understanding of what the project entails. You'll find project postings for things like 25 articles about credit repair, a white paper on safely traveling to the Bahamas, or a posting about many articles on different topics.

Once a subject line catches your attention, click on it and read the details. This is where you'll find the projected deadlines and price ranges, as well as a more in-depth description of the job. If the project appeals to you and you want to place a bid, wait because there is one more step you should take first.

Click on the client's name and find your way to their ratings page. If you find that they have even a few negative ratings left by other writers, skip over the project and do not place a bid. Trust me, you're not going to be the writer to finally please this buyer. Next, click on the writer's pages that left the negative ratings and see what kind of feedback the buyer left for them. Now, imagine your own rating page with that type of feedback on it. Are you sweating yet?

Good, and a little fear in this area is a good and necessary thing.

Remember, there are some serial complainers out there, and you should do whatever you can to avoid them. One bad rating on your feedback page can and will put a serious dent in your business.

Okay, the project sounds interesting, the buyer checks out, now it's time to place the bid. There's one thing you need to understand here, bidding is an art. If you approach it as such, you will see the success and growth of your business, provided that you always submit timely and professional work.

On the other hand, if you take a scattered approach to bidding, you'll reap a scattered result. And that's no way to build an Empire.

Think of a bid in four parts: the personalization, the push, the big easy, and the follow-up. Here they are, broken down individually.

The Personalization

You've heard the saying that people like to do business with people they like. It's true. That philosophy may be even truer for writers because buyers tend to want, well... personality in their writer's work. So it stands to reason that the kiss of death to a bid is a dry, punctual, and practical style. Instead, you've got to make your words jump off the page and grab the buyer's attention. The easiest way to do that is to personalize it from the get go. Using our example project posting, your personalized opening might look something like this:

> Dear buyer,
> "As an avid gardener (Organic of course-is there really any other way?), I was thrilled to find your job posting. I would love to be considered for this project."

In this opening, you've established yourself as an expert, clearly aligned your gardening values with the buyers, and told him that you are eager to take on the project. That ought to get their attention, huh?

The Push

Next, you're going to have to sell yourself. I know, most writers have a major problem with this. That's because so many of us are introverts and calling attention to ourselves doesn't come naturally, but if you want your Empire to succeed, it's a skill you'll have to develop.

You know you could do a wonderful job for the buyer, but he doesn't yet realize it. And it's your job to make him understand. Again using our organic gardening sample posting, here is an example of the push:

> "I've been a full-time freelance writer for some time, and have produced hundreds of top notch articles for my clients. Here's what some of them have to say about my work:
> "Working with Crank 'Em Out Writing Services was the best business decision I ever made."

> "The keyword articles Crank 'Em Out Writing Services did for me have drastically increased the traffic to my site."

Did you notice how the writer bragged about his accomplishments? That's okay. Did you see how he tooted his own horn? Perfectly acceptable. Shamelessly promoted himself? Uh-huh. You have to admit that the writer sounds like a pretty good bet for that project, doesn't he?

Precisely.

The Big Easy

You now have the attention of the buyer, and have made it clear why he should hire you. Now you've got to get them to take that next step and grant you the job. How do you do that? By making it easy for them. Let me give you an example:

> My bid for your project is $25.00 per article, totaling $500 for the entire project. Your two week deadline suits my schedule, and that includes time for revisions in case you require them. I work tirelessly to please my clients, and can guarantee that you will walk away satisfied with your product. To get an idea of my writing style, you can view my portfolio on this site, or go to my website (be sure to include a link) for an expanded collection of my work.
>
> In addition, if you have any questions for me, simply send me a message and I will respond immediately.

I look forward to working with you,
Crank 'Em Out Writing Services

You see? You were clear in your pricing and deadline availability, and then you let him know that he won't be stuck with articles he doesn't want. You put him at ease about the type of writer he would be working with. Then you gave him a link so he'd have easy access to your portfolio on the bid site as well as the one on your own web site. Finally, you made yourself available for any questions the buyer might have.

How easy is that?

The Follow Up

Are you ready to ensure that you're a project magnet? Remember, the day after you send the bid, you should go back to the project posting and send a follow up note to the buyer. It's okay to get creative with your message because the purpose of it is to get your name in front of the buyer again.

There, now you've done absolutely everything you can to increase your chances of winning the bid. At this point, the buyer may contact you to try and negotiate different prices or to talk about strategy or topics for their project, but either way, you are on your way.

Now that we've covered how to place a bid in detail, let's talk about other aspects of the process you need to know.

The Best Way to Conduct Research

We've already covered the basic format of all the common types of Internet content you will be asked to write. But before you begin, you must prepare. If you're an experienced writer, you may be scrunching together your eyebrows and thinking you should skip over this section. Maybe you're right. But remember that you'll be writing a staggering amount of articles in three months and you might need some help organizing your time to accomplish it. Let me show you how I did it.

Most writer's inclination is to research one article at a time, but then again, most of them aren't writing 10 articles a day, plus running a business. The key to sanity during this busy time is to condense as much of your research efforts as you can. Luckily, when you're assigned a project, it's generally for a batch of articles on the same topic. Knowing this, you can do most of your research for each project in one swoop.

Let's use our organic gardening project as an example. You've been assigned 10 articles on the topic, so where do you start? The starting point of any bulk article assignment should be the topic research. If you're familiar with the subject, list as many article ideas as you can that would need little to no research. (Keep in mind that some clients will give you the article titles, so you won't have to come up with them yourself, but many won't.) If I were assigned 10 articles about this topic, my list of article ideas might look something like this:

1. Organic gardening and containers: are the two compatible?

2. Container gardening and possible toxins
3. How to control weeds with container gardening
4. How to keep the pests out of your container garden naturally
5. The benefits of organic gardening
6. Teach your children how to garden organically
7. How much sun does your container garden need?
8. What can you grow in containers?
9. Growing herbs organically in containers
10. How to ensure your container dirt is chemical free

I could write intelligently on this topic without a lot of research, but what if I were assigned articles I knew nothing about? How would I get ideas for topics on say, the latest advances in stem cell procedures? By getting online. By simply typing "stem cell procedures" into a search engine, I would come up with a wealth of information that could easily inspire topic ideas for the articles.

By doing all of your research for similar topics at once, you'll save hours of time. Save even more time by keeping an open document where you cut and paste all of the URLs for the research you'll want to go back to and read for each topic.

Submitting Your Work

You've finished the articles and are ready to submit them to the client. The process will vary, depending on the site you're using. On most sites you will upload your work as attachments and send them in a message to the buyer. Your message should look something like this:

> Mr. Charlie Client,
>
> I've finished your project, and have attach the articles to this message. I sincerely enjoyed working with you, and hope that we can do so again in the near future. Please keep in mind that I do all types of writing such as e-books, newsletters, white papers, and website contact, so don't hesitate to contact me for future work. Meanwhile, I wish you all the best and incredible success with your website.
>
> Best,
>
> One smart writer

Now attach the articles and push send.

Getting Paid

If you are using a bid site, you won't have to do anything to get paid. Once the client approves your work, they will release the funds. Each site gives buyers a set amount of time to release the funds after the work has been approved. Get to know the rules for each bid site you work on.

On the other hand, if you are working with a client you didn't find on a bid site, you will need to create an invoice at this point and e-mail it to them. Most clients will prefer to pay you via PayPal, so you should include your PayPal e-mail address on your invoice.

In the event that the client wants to pay you with a check or direct deposit, simply provide them with the information so they can.

How to Navigate the Ratings System

Your last step of the process is to give your client a rating. There are two schools of thought on this subject. Some writers go ahead and rate their client right away, hoping that their client will see the positive rating and will be inclined to reciprocate with a similar rating.

Others take a more cautious approach and wait to post their rating until after the buyer has posted his. Their theory is that the buyer doesn't want a bad rating any more than they do, so they hold back their rating as insurance. Personally, I play it by ear, depending on my interactions with the client throughout the project.

That's it, you've now completed a project from start to finish. Whew! Wait... why are you still sitting there? Don't you have another project to get started on?

The Four Must-Do's for Success

Before we move on to the next chapter, I want to talk to you about four things you must do while building your Empire in order to achieve success. If you do these four things consistently, I guarantee you that you will be miles ahead of your competition.

- **Pace yourself**. Yes, your schedule will be crazy, but that doesn't mean you don't have to pace yourself. Remember, slow and steady builds the Empire.

- **Over compensate.** You're building your reputation so be sure to go that extra mile on every project you do.

- **Don't over commit.** Be sure you never take on more than you can do. If in doubt, negotiate a longer deadline before you accept the project.

- **Never miss a deadline.** Ever. I don't care if it takes staying up all night three days in a row, don't do it. It's the kiss of death for a writer in this type of business.

Empire Builders Arch Enemy #6:
A Lack of Discipline

Running a writing Empire isn't for sissies. If you
don't stay disciplined, especially in the early stages of
building, your Empire will fall flat on its face. Period.
So, make up your mind to suck it up no matter how
difficult it gets. And then do whatever it takes to
make it a success.

CHAPTER 8:

Expanding Your Empire: Making Your First Hire

By this time in the building process, you should have more work than you can comfortably handle. It's time to bring in your first writer. While this is the most exciting time of your growing Empire, it's also the time when you will be at your most vulnerable.

You will no longer be solely responsible for the success of your business because your employee's actions and talent will have a direct impact on it. Knowing that, wouldn't you agree that caution should be your ruling theme? I know, you've been working crazy hours for months now and you just want to throw half of your work load onto someone else.

But think of it like this: you've been working crazy hours for weeks now, and it's your job to make sure it wasn't all for naught. Trust me, relief is on its way, but let's make sure we move ahead cautiously in this critical junction of the building process. I want you to remember something throughout the hiring process. The decisions you are about to make could launch your Empire into the stratosphere, or bring the walls crumbling down. You'd better make a cup of Joe, we've got some strategizing to do.

Creating a Help Wanted Posting

The right help wanted posting is crucial for two reasons. First, you want to make sure to attract the type of writer who will help make your business successful. By clearly stating your requirements up front, it will weed out all of the unqualified writers. Secondly, a proper posting will save you time. And you certainly realize by now just how important that is.

Here is a sample help wanted posting. Read it, and then we will dissect it together.

> Are You Looking for Part-Time Writing Work?
> I need an article writer who can produce 5 to 10 articles per day. I pay on average of $10.00 per article, depending on experience. If interested, please submit three writing samples to.... Please, only native English speakers. All work will be checked for plagiarism before payment is made.

The first part of the ad makes it clear that the position being offered is part time. This will eliminate a bunch of applicants who are only interested in full-time work, and that will save you time in the review process. The second and third sentences clarify exactly what the potential writer would be doing for you, and what your volume expectations are. The fourth sentence lets the applicants get a pretty good

SAM KERNS

idea of how much income they could make by working for you.

In the next sentence, you are letting applicants from other countries know that you want only native English speakers. If you don't include this phrase, you will be inundated by applicants from other countries who, quite frankly, may not have a strong grasp on the English language. Keep in mind that many people hire writers from other countries, but unless you have a firm grasp on grammar and possess above average editing skills, it's probably not a good idea.

Plagiarism is the number one enemy of your Empire, and unfortunately, you will have writers who submit plagiarized work to you. It's the nature of the business, but it will be your job to catch it. I will talk more about this later, but mentioning the fact that their work will be checked in your ad will eliminate many of the worst offenders.

Finally, the ad gives the applicant some very specific instructions to follow when submitting an application. This will tell you which applicants are prone to following your directions and which are not. I make it a rule that if the applicant fails to attach the requested samples, I won't even consider hiring them.

Of course, you'll want to tailor your ad to your particular needs, but hopefully this sample ad will steer you in the right direction. Now let's take a look at where to place your ads.

Placing Your Ads

You'll want to ensure that your ad is placed on a website where the most qualified writers will find it. Let me explain what I mean by qualified. You're not looking for a writer with years of experience or one who has a portfolio filled with articles they've written for top notch markets. Those types of writers are able to land high paying jobs on their own and won't be likely to work for what you're offering.

Instead, you need writers who are good at their trade, but don't enjoy the process of looking for work. You would be surprised how many qualified writers there are who simply don't have the skills or desire to look for work on a consistent basis. These are the writers who would accept less per article in exchange for a constant flow of work, and that's why they will fit into your Empire perfectly.

Remember, the Empire you're building is a means to an end. It's a way to make a great living while eventually having enough time to work on those things that are most special to you. But to your employees, it will be a job. So your best bet will be to place your help wanted posting at sites where beginning writers and people looking to work from home hang out. I gave you a list of places to find projects earlier, and you will find the majority of your writers on those sites. Here are some additional sites that you should use to find your writers.

Freelance Writer's Den. Here, you can sign up to create an employer profile, and then submit a job posting. You'll even be able to request writers with specialty category skills if you choose.

Indeed.com. You can search by job type and even narrow it down to a particular area if you want. This site aggregates job postings from all across the country.

Writer Access. This site is full of freelance writers looking for work, and while the prices vary, you can find writers for as low as 2 cents per word, or about

$10 for a 500 word article. While you won't be able to post a help wanted listing here, you can search out writers on your own.

WAHM.com. This is a site that's geared toward moms who want to work from home. They offer a section where you can post jobs for writers.

Your First Contact

You can tell a lot from a writer's first contact with you. From the way they communicate with you to the samples they include in their application, you'll be able to discern whether or not the writer would be beneficial to your business.

Pay attention to the tone of the e-mail. Is it friendly and helpful or does it give the impression that they're doing you a favor by applying for the job? Are there misspellings throughout the content or have they edited and proofread the e-mail the way you hope they will their articles? Did they follow the specific instructions you gave in the job posting? For example, if you asked them to send 3 samples, did they only send 1? If you asked them to paste the samples in the body of the e-mail, did they do it? Or did they ignore your instructions and attach them as files? It's all significant and will likely foreshadow your working relationship with them.

Next check out the applicant's writing samples. Some, you'll be able to immediately rule out because of style or grammar concerns. You have a unique style of writing, and your best bet will be to find a writer whose style closely resembles yours. This will make it easier to split up large projects between the two of you. Once you have a good style match, you can branch out and hire other writers with the ability to do things you can't, such as write about different topics or in a style you're not comfortable with, such as humor.

Be sure to run each and every sample through your plagiarism software so you can be sure the applicant wrote it. Never skip this step. You would be amazed at the writers out there who resort to this ugly practice.

Once you narrow down the applicants, it's time for a little one-on-one communication. Let's see what they're made of, shall we? Your e-mail to the potential writers should look something like this:

Dear writer,

I received your e-mail and samples, and am pleased at what I saw. You're a talented writer, and I'd like to discuss the possibility of you doing some work for me. But first, I have some questions. Would you mind sending me the answers at your earliest convenience?

What is the minimum and maximum amount of articles you can write per day?

How long have you been writing internet articles?

What are your favorite topics to write about? Least favorite?

Are you available for rush jobs?

Are you available for other types of projects such as white papers, e-books, sales letters, and more?

I look forward to your response, and I'll be talking to you soon.

By asking the writer these questions, along with any others you decide to include, you should be able to make an informed hiring decision. You'll likely go back and forth with several writers, and may need to send follow up questions before you can make a final decision.

The next step is difficult because you're going to have to choose just one of the writers. Yes, I know, you have three great applicants and there is no possible way you can just choose just one. Your wheels are already spinning, aren't they? You're thinking of dividing up the work two or three ways so you can grab all of the writers before they get away.

Listen to me. No, I mean really listen. Don't do it. If you do, you'll end up with three disappointed, hungry writers instead of one loyal worker who will grow with you as your Empire expands. Instead, pick one and send an e-mail to the others telling them that, although you're not hiring them this time, you will contact them shortly when you intend to hire again.

Okay, you've made your decision. Congratulations, you're now officially an Empire ruler. Let's talk about the details.

What to Pay

By now you should have a good estimate of what your average income is per article. As I stated at the beginning of this book, typical pay rates for a 500 word article range between $5.00 and $50.00. Depending on the price range you've decided to concentrate on, your average price will fall somewhere in between. I'll use $25.00 in my discussions because that's the most common rate.

When deciding what to pay your writers, it's important to keep a few facts in mind. They are:

- The amount must be enough to make them want to keep working for you.

- You must make enough to cover your overhead, taxes, and still earn a profit.

It's a fine balance, I know. You're the one who will spend countless hours scouring the job postings, negotiating with clients, maintaining your online portfolio and pages on all the bid sites, checking all articles for plagiarism, as well as editing each and every article before it's sent to the client. In addition, you will be the one who runs the risk of not being paid. On the other hand, the writer will research and write the articles. So how do you make it fair?

The formula I've found best is a 60/40 split, with 60 percent going to you. Using this formula, you would pay a writer $10.00 on a $25.00 article, and keep $15.00 for yourself. If the writer is able to produce 10 articles per day, they would earn $100 per day, $500 per week, or $2000 per month. That's pretty good income for a writer who never has to seek out new jobs. Your take at $15.00 per article would be $150 per day, $750 per week, or $3000 per month. This formula is fair to both parties because each is earning the right amount of money for the work involved.

Of course, you'll have other projects that consist of e-books, white papers, and more, but if you stick to the 60/40 role for all of them, you'll find that the writer will be happy, your expenses will be covered, and you'll earn a handsome profit.

SAM KERNS

How to Pay Your Writers

Because your writers will be hired online, work online, and communicate with you online, they will also expect to be paid online. There are several good online payment services, but the one that seems to be global and most readily accepted is PayPal. I've used it for years and have never had a writer object to being paid this way. Simply tell them that this is how you pay and ask them to set up their own account, if they don't already have one.

Rather than paying per job (talk about time consuming!), pick a day like Friday and called it payday. I've found that it's a pretty good motivator to make it a policy to only pay for the articles that were due that week once they've been turned in. (By the payday deadline. I've always used 5 P.M. Friday as my deadline.) In other words, if a writer doesn't have all that week's articles in by 5 O'clock on Friday, the ones they turn in after that go on next week's invoice. This does two things. First, it prevents you from having to spend Friday night or the weekend working on a tardy writer's edits, and secondly, it shows the writers that you're serious about your deadlines.

Keep in mind that your writers are independent contractors and not employees. We will get into this fully later in this chapter, but for now you should know that you should never issue a payment to a writer until they have submitted a detailed invoice to you.

In addition to following the law for independent contractors, insisting on a detailed invoice before issuing payment will give both you and the writer a record of payment in order to avoid any confusion as to whether or not a project has been paid for.

114

That's the basics of paying your writers. Let's take a look at some specifics of this industry as it pertains to payment.

Asking for Deposits

Depending on whether you are working with a client on a bid site or on your own you may be wise to ask for a deposit up front. The bid sites will require buyers to deposit the amount of the project into an escrow account, so you don't have to worry about getting paid from them. But if you are working with a client outside of a bid site, you might want to ask for a deposit. Not all writers do, but if you are doing a large project for a new client that you've never done business with before, it's not unrealistic to ask for a quarter of the amount up front, another quarter when you're halfway through the project, and the remainder once you've turned in the work. Of course, once you and the client develop a relationship over many jobs, you may feel comfortable not asking them for a deposit. It's up to you, but remember that if you don't get paid, your writer will still expect to.

Considering that you may require deposits up front from some of your clients, what about your writers? Should you also pay them a deposit? Let me ask you a question: will you most likely get the fastest and best work from your writer by paying them half up front, or keeping the entire fee until they've turned in their work? If that seems cold-hearted, imagine yourself trying to explain to your buyer why the project is late, or better yet, imagine yourself on the eve of the deadline pulling an all-nighter because you're already paid writer didn't come through.

Now, there are exceptions to this rule. If you assign

a writer a time-consuming project, such as an e-book, it's unrealistic to expect them to go a lengthy period of time without getting paid. But you still don't want to pay them up front. Instead, plan to pay them half of their fee once they've submitted half of the project, and the balance when they submit the final half.

Once you become familiar with your writers and develop a long-term relationship with them things might look different. I have worked with some of my writers for years, and over those years I've given them advances when they were in a bind, and have made exceptions on the Friday deadline for payment. I would never do that for a new writer, but over time, I have developed trusting relationships with some of my writers, and I feel that it's in both of our interests to work together.

Now, let's continue with more of the basics for employing writers.

The Ins and Outs of Scheduling Assignments

You will be responsible for determining which assignments you will keep for yourself and which assignments to give to your writer, or writers as time goes on. Over time, you will come to know which topics your writers excel in, and which ones they need more experience in. This is important to you because the more proficient they are at a topic, the more they can produce, and the less editing you will have to do.

But in the beginning, you'll have to rely on the answers from the writer's interview questions. Remember those? One of the questions you asked was which topics they were most and least interested in writing.

In the beginning, use this as a guide and assign them the articles they're most comfortable writing, keeping the remainder of them for yourself. Over time, you can begin to assign them new topics, increasing the amount of work they do for you.

Now some of you may be thinking that any writer worth his salt should be able to research and write an article about anything, right? That's true, but most writers aren't trying to produce 10 articles a day.

By keeping your writers grouped into specific topics, you'll save them some serious research time. Here is an example of how your Empire assignment status will look in time:

Writer # 1:
art, interior design, home repair

Writer #2:
children, family fun

Writer #3:
product descriptions, creative pieces, sales letters

Writer #4:
business, insurance, entrepreneurship, IT

Writer #5:
gardening, foodie stuff, humor, pets

There are dozens of other relevant topics, but this chart gives you an idea of how your topic assignments should be done.

Your ultimate goal should be to cross train your writers. For instance, your family life writer should be eased into articles about pets, and the pet writer should begin producing some family life articles. This will ensure that you are never without an expert on the hot topics.

In addition to categorizing the writer's topics, you'll also need to take into consideration the writer's time and schedule. Remember, most writers won't be as ambitious as you and they won't want to work crazy hours. They will want to work a normal 6 to 8 hours a day. Some will want to write in the morning, while others do their best work at night.

This can come into play for certain projects. For example, if you win a project that requires 200 articles in a week, you obviously won't be able to assign them all to the same writer. In the beginning, you'll take on some of them, but after you've hired more writers, you'll be able to split the project among them.

Juggling your writer's schedules is an art and you will have to learn it quickly. Once you do, it will make your life much easier. I use a white board next to my desk with my writer's names and job assignments underneath them. I also indicate the dates that the assignments are due. I'm in a visual person and I like to be able to glance at my white board as I'm working throughout the day. But I realize that many of you would do better with a spreadsheet. That's fine. The key is to have the information at your fingertips so you can check it periodically throughout the day. This will allow you to add projects to each writer's schedule easily. It will also prevent you from being caught off guard if a writer is nearing a deadline and hasn't yet submitted anything.

Speaking of deadlines, let's talk about how you can avoid having your writers miss them.

Performing Periodic Progress Reports

Imagine this: two weeks ago you assigned one of your writers 80 articles. The deadline is tomorrow, so you drop your writer a note asking them what time you can expect the articles. After all, you still have to edit them and check for plagiarism. You've allowed yourself a few days to do this task before you have to turn them in to the client. Then the unthinkable happens. You receive an email that sounds something like this:

> Dear boss,
>
> I'm so sorry but my little girl was hospitalized last week and I haven't even looked at or thought about these articles. I am so sorry, I feel horrible! Please forgive me. Can I contact you when things calm down around here?

Is your heart thumping in your chest? Is there cold sweat on your upper lip at the thought of something like this happening? There should be, because unfortunately it happens all the time.

But here's the good news. That <u>never</u> has to happen to you. Ever. Here's how you can prevent it: periodic progress reports.

Rather than have your writers submit the entire project once it's completed, instruct them to submit their completed work at the end of each day. For example, if a project consist of 50 articles, the writer assigned to that project should submit 10 articles to you at the end of every day.

Not only will this prevent you from being caught short on a deadline, it will allow you ample time to reassign the project if the writer falls through. Don't only do this on large jobs, but also the small ones. Remember, the purpose is to make sure that the work is being done, and it will also make it easier for you to edit, give guidance, and check it for plagiarism because you can do it at the end of every day instead of all at once.

The Issue of Bylines

Admit it, most of us writers are big heads and we want credit for everything we do, even if it's just a 500 word internet article about socks. The bad news is that you won't be able to offer your writers bylines. In other words they will produce thousands and thousands of words and not get credit for even one of them. Most experienced writers understand this, but if you hire new writers, they might have a problem with it. You should spell this out clearly when you hire someone so it won't become an issue later.

How Can You Protect Your Client's Identity?

This very question used to keep me up at night. After all, couldn't one of my writers just enter a few lines of an article they did for you into a search engine, find the article and thus the web site that it was written for, and then email the client directly?

Yes.

And if they can do that, couldn't they offer to work directly for the client, cutting you and your Empire out of the deal?

Yes.

But wouldn't that mean a loss of income?

Yes.

It's difficult for an Empire ruler to let go of even an inch of your Empire, isn't it? But the reality is a not-so-scrupulous writer could do just that. In fact, it's happened to me. Once. Fortunately I learned some things you can do to protect your hard built Empire, and I'm happy to pass them along to you.

- Don't assign all of a repeat buyers work to one writer. If you do, that will give the writer a sense of security with that client. This happens when the writer knows he's doing a good amount of work for one client. Your writer may begin to think that they could survive on work from only that one client, especially if they cut out your portion of the fee. Combat this by making sure your client's work is distributed among yourself and a few different writers.

- Make sure your relationships with your clients are solid. Don't forget to keep up a consistent and friendly flow of communication with them. Remember them on holidays and give them the occasional deal. This will build loyalty, which would make it more difficult for them to cut you out and work with the writer, should the opportunity arise.

- Make sure your writers understand your special relationship with your clients. This can be done every now and then while talking with the writer about a job via e-mail. Sentences such as "I've worked with this client for many years, and I know what he wants," will help the writer understand that you have a tight relationship with your clients. If they know this, they won't be so quick to try and cut you out for fear of being rejected by the client and losing their gig with you. I've seen other books suggest that you have the writers sign a non-compete contract, but since they are working as an independent contractor, you can't legally ask them to do that. And if you do, the IRS may reclassify them as an employee and force you to pay them as an employee.

- Finally, one of the most important steps you can take is to use an entirely different e-mail address and name when dealing with your writers. Remember, bids are public and what you don't want is your writer seeing your name and email address on bid sites. If they're able to find that, they'll have information about who your clients are and how much you're paid for projects. Instead, use one e-mail and name for your buyer, and a nickname and different e-mail address for your writers.

Should You Hire Overseas Help?

In order to put together a well written article in English, it's necessary to have a grasp on the language. Unfortunately, that doesn't always happen when dealing with writers whose native language isn't English. Obviously there are always exceptions, but as a general rule, the work typically isn't up to snuff.

So, why would anybody want to hire a non-native

speaker? It all comes down to money. Because the cost of living is so much lower in some countries, the writers there are able to work for less. Considerably less. But that lower payment comes with a price: much more editing for you. It's not unheard of for an editor to have to almost rewrite an entire article written by a non-native English speaker. So, you have to decide how much your time is worth. Just remember, the quality of the articles that you send to clients can never be compromised. You are the Empire ruler, and are ultimately responsible for every word you submit.

Taxes and Your Writers

The writers that you hire are not permanent employees, but are considered independent contractors which means that they take on assignments from you and as many other people as they can handle. When using independent contractors, you are not allowed to dictate how or when they complete their work. For example, you cannot tell them they have to work between nine and five. In other words, they are self-employed and are doing projects for you.

Because they are independent contractors and not employees, you are not responsible for withholding taxes from their pay. At the end of the year, you are required to send them a 1099 form which states the amount of money you paid them that year. You will also send a copy of this form to the IRS at the end of the year when you submit your own taxes.

We've been on quite a journey, haven't we? By now, you are at least four months into your new Empire. How does it feel? The great news is that your

Empire is still in its infancy and you will determine how big you want it to grow. Let's move on to our final chapter and we'll talk about expanding your Empire.

Empire Builders Arch Enemy #7: Not Setting the Right Tone with Your Writers

Your writers will be the lifeblood of your business, and it's important to set the right tone initially and carry it throughout your working relationship. No one wants to work for someone who is a constant grouch or makes unrealistic demands, and neither will your writers. But on the other hand, if you're too nice or accommodating, your writers will walk all over you and create unnecessary drama and problems for you.

You'll need to find the right balance between professionalism and niceness. It may take some trial and error, but once you get it, your life will become so much easier.

CHAPTER 9:

Don't Stop!
Take Your Empire
to the Next Level.

About a month after you hire your new writer, you should have a pretty good rhythm going and a little more time on your hands. Your writer should be comfortable producing 10 articles per day, and you should know which areas they do best in. It feels good to have a little breathing room, doesn't it?

Guess what? The break's over. It's time to pick up the pace again and hire another writer. That means you should begin now by increasing your outgoing bids in preparation for the new writer. You should also place another help wanted posting and start narrowing down your choices. If you found a good writer the last time you placed an ad, you might want to contact them now.

By now, you have a good idea of what is lacking as far as topic areas. Maybe you're winning a lot of bids on model trains, but neither you nor your writer know a lot about them. Knowing this will help you in your search for a new writer.

Once you've made your second hire, you should follow the same procedure that you did with the first one and nurture them along until they are producing 10 articles a day. Once this writer is up to speed, you should be earning about $6000 a month.

Continue to follow this process and add another writer as soon as your newest writer is up to speed. How many writers you hire is up to you, and it will all depend on how much income you desire to make. Once you reach the point where you feel you are at your limit, you will have two choices, and what you do next will determine the type of Empire you have. Let's take a look at both of your choices.

Keeping the Status Quo

There is a good majority of you whose thinking goes something like this: Hey, I've got 3 writers working for me now, and each produce enough articles to earn me a great income. Why in the world would I want to mess with that?

And you would be right. In the beginning of this book, I told you that I would show you how to earn $100,000 a year running a writing business. We've reached that point, and I realize that some of you will be satisfied with just that. Congratulations, you've built a profitable Empire that should serve you well for years to come.

But I also know there is another segment of you that hear a persistent whisper in the back of their minds. It says: What's next? Surely if I can go this far, I can do more. You've had a taste of success, and now you want to build an even bigger Empire. You want an Empire that has no boundaries. You want to rule the writing business world.

This next section is for you.

Go on to Rule the World

The easiest way to expand your Empire is to increase the number of projects that you handle. But that would mean you would have to hire more writers, and it may not be realistic to think that you'll be able to handle them all, plus do everything else that comes with running such a large business. It all comes back to our first problem, time.

So, how do you find the time to take on increased responsibilities? You hire a freelance editor, that's how. Here's how to do it.

A freelance editor will work on an article-by-article basis. In other words, you will pay her a set amount for every article she edits and checks for plagiarism. Ideally, your editor will quickly be able to handle all of your monthly articles. That will free you up to work on hiring and managing more writers, as well as keep up with clients and new job searches. You should plan on paying a freelance editor approximately $2.50 per article, which will bring down your profit per article. But the increased sales will more than make up for it.

You can find a freelance editor on the same sites where you found your freelance writers. Run a help wanted posting just like you did with your writers, and make sure to give them a couple of test assignments to make sure they're good enough.

Of course you can continue this cycle by hiring another editor as soon as this one has reached her capacity. You will eventually reach a point where you cannot keep up with job bidding and client communications, and at this point you may need to hire an assistant and train them to take over some of your duties.

Now, do me a favor. Sit back and close your eyes and imagine this scene: you are the ruler of an Empire of your own making. Blood, sweat, and tears went into the construction of your kingdom. Because you were intimately involved with the building process, you know every stone, every doorway, and every aspect of your kingdom. Take the scepter in your hands and lean back into the richness of your throne. You are a good ruler, a fair ruler, and a just one. Your subjects are loyal and work hard for you because they trust you to always do what's right and fair. You have earned your place as a ruler, but know this: your enemies (the competition), will try and take it all away from you.

They will lay siege to your Empire and attempt to lead your subjects into a revolt. But aside from being a good and just ruler, you are also smart. Here are a few tips that will help you protect your Empire from enemy attacks.

Know your Weak Areas

When an enemy decides to attack, and they will, it will be for one of these reasons: to eliminate the competition (that would be you), to steal your writers, or to take away your clients. But if you know this, you can reinforce those areas so that the enemy won't stand a chance when they come up against you. Let's look at all three areas of vulnerability and discuss the various ways you can reinforce them.

Arch Enemy Attack #1: Eliminate the Competition (You)

Remember this, every project bid that you win is one less that your competition has for themselves. And if you are doing the amount of business that we've talked about in this book, you've taken a good chunk of change from the competition. And many of them won't take too kindly to that. In fact, some of your competitors may try and take down your Empire. But if you make certain that you do everything you're supposed to do on every job, the chances of that happening are minuscule.

Here is your enemy repellent checklist. Learn it and do it on every job because the one time you skip any of the steps will be the time the enemy has tried to set you up. How will they set you up? By hiring you on a small job with the intention of giving you a bad rating, or by getting themselves hired by you and then submitting poorly written plagiarized work at the last minute for a large job. Does that sound too farfetched? It's happened to me. Here's how to counter these types of attacks as best as you can:

- Verify the samples submitted on a writer's application were really written by them.

- Make your writers submit to the progress checks we discussed. This will prevent the last minute sabotage.

- Never skip a plagiarism check.

- Always edit articles before you turn them in.

- Check buyer profiles to be certain they don't have a habit of leaving bad ratings.

- Never hire another writing company to do your work. I've seen people do this, and it usually ends in disaster.

- If you do get an unfair rating on a good job, protest it. The bid sites will usually protect you if you been unfairly rated.

In short, if you do everything I've taught you in this book as you run your company, the enemy won't have anything to sabotage you with.

Arch Enemy Attack #2: Steal Your Employees

You put a lot of time and effort into hiring the best freelance writers out there. Guess what? Your enemies would do anything to steal them away from you. Sometimes your competition will try and steal them, and sadly sometimes your clients will try to hire your writers out from under you. Here are a few strategies to prevent that from happening.

- Keep your writers completely separated from each other. You don't ever want them communicating with each other. That means you shouldn't send out bulk emails to them and never give out their names to each other.

- Keep your client's names from the writers, and the writers' names from your clients. No one needs to know that information but you.

- Do not give your writers a byline. If you do, it would be too easy for someone to contact them on their own.

- Be sure to use one e-mail address and name for communicating with your writers and a separate name and address for your clients and the bid sites. Under no circumstances should these two names and e-mail accounts ever cross.

- Make sure that you always pay a fair wage. Prices will change and you need to keep up with the current market pay rate. Remember, your writers probably have a family to support, too.

- If a writer does an outstanding job on a difficult project, give them a bonus. If they've never missed a deadline, reward them. Everyone wants to feel appreciated and letting your writers know that they are is one of the best ways to build loyalty.

Remember, your writers are a critical aspect of your Empire. By treating them well and paying them a good wage, you will elicit loyalty in them so that when the enemy attacks and tries to steal them from you, they will remain loyal to you.

Arch Enemy Attack #3: Stealing Your Clients

When building your Empire, one of your biggest goals is to build up a base of clients who come to you again and again with projects. I've had clients give me hundreds of articles each and every month, as well as projects that turned into monthly blogs or high-end online newsletters. These types of clients will be the foundation of your Empire, and your competition will likely lie awake at night trying to figure out how to get their grubby little hands on them. You must protect them at all costs. Here's how to do that:

- Never reveal a client's name or contact information to anyone. Not to your writers, your editor, or your best friend. That would be like Colonel Sanders publishing his secret sauce recipe on the Internet.

- Never give the name of a client to another client.

- Make sure your clients stay loyal to you by always delivering well-researched, perfectly written articles on time. Make sure they know that you or your editor approve every article before it is turned in.

- Occasionally give your clients an appreciation discount out of the blue.

- Never give your clients the name of your writers.

- If a client tells you that a writer has approached them directly, immediately stop giving that writer work and let your other clients know what's happening. Be sure they understand that before you submit any writer's work it has been polished and checked for plagiarism by you.

- Make sure one writer never does all of the work for one client. Mix it up and keep everyone guessing.

If you take all of these precautions consistently, your Empire should thrive and you will enjoy many years doing what you love. Ah, yes that reminds me. We have one more area to cover on our journey, don't we? And I bet you thought I forgot.

Doing What You Love

At this critical juncture, you have a choice. Remember how I asked you to create a list of your goals and priorities at the beginning of the book? Unless your number one goal is to make a lot of money, there are other things in your life that you want to accomplish. I don't know what they are because everyone's are different, but let's imagine that your number one goal is to have the time to write a book.

We started out with the premise that only 10 percent of writers could actually make a real living at it, didn't we? We talked about the fact that for some of us, writing novels or bestselling nonfiction books was our dream, but we couldn't figure out how to do it. After all, one person can only write so much, and after you've written what you have to in order to make ends meet, there just aren't a lot of creative juices left, are there?

But now things have changed. You probably have four or five writers working for you, which means you should have reached your financial goal. You are finally at the place that, if you want to, you can take a serious stab at writing that book that's been bouncing around in your head all these years. How? Watch and learn.

Did you know that most novelists work on average of four hours per day on their books? Others write just 1,000 to 2,000 words a day in order to complete a book in a couple of months. While that sounds easy, when you have a full schedule, that small commitment can seem overwhelming, can't it?

But how much time do you think would open up if you hired an editor to handle your writer's work and then, instead of growing your Empire more by continuing to hire more and more writers, you simply stopped construction on your Empire so you could concentrate on your other priorities? Now that's not to say that you should hand over the keys to your Empire to someone else, but by limiting how much you grow, you should easily be able to carve out an extra few hours in your day to pursue your other dreams, whether that's writing a book, spending more time with your kids, or finally packaging and mass producing those wonderful brownies you make.

And if you decide later on that you want to continue growing your Empire, there would be no reason not to pick up where you left off. After all, it's your baby, and you hold the keys in your hands.

Conclusion

Well, that brings us to the end our journey. I hope this book has inspired you and caused you to realize that building a writing business isn't really possible unless you expand it beyond yourself.

One of the lessons I had to learn the hard way is that it's a big world out there and we can easily limit ourselves by dreaming too small. Instead, when we **dream big** and set our sights on the **big goal**, we are better able to reach it.

So, my hope for you is that you set your goals high and work until you reach them!

My next book, How to Start a Home-Based Food Business: Turn Your Foodie Dreams into Serious Income (Work from Home Series: Book 3), will be released in a few short months. Sign up at my website, RainMakerPress.com, and I'll send you a quick email when it's released.

And **please**, if you found this book helpful, please let other readers know by leaving a review.

Until then, get out there and make your dreams come true!

Sam

Made in the USA
Middletown, DE
25 August 2016